D0646197

JULIA COOPER

THE LAST WORD

REVIVING THE DYING ART OF EULOGY

COACH HOUSE BOOKS, TORONTO

Canada Council **Conseil des Arts**
for the Arts du Canada

Published with the generous assistance of the Canada Council for the Arts and the Ontario Arts Council. Coach House Books also gratefully acknowledges the support of the Government of Canada through the Canada Book Fund and the Government of Ontario through the Ontario Book Publishing Tax Credit.

LIBRARY AND ARCHIVES CANADA CATALOGUING IN PUBLICATION

Cooper, Julia, 1985-, author
     The last word : reviving the dying art of eulogy / Julia Cooper.

(Exploded views)
Issued in print and electronic formats.
ISBN 978-1-55245-341-4 (softcover).

     1. Eulogies. 2. Eulogies--History and criticism. I. Title. II. Series: Exploded views

GT3390.c67 2017   393   c2017-900538-3

The Last Word is available as an ebook: ISBN 978 1 77056 501 2 (EPUB), ISBN 978 1 77056 502 9 (PDF).

Purchase of the print version of this book entitles you to a free digital copy. To claim your ebook of this title, please email sales@chbooks.com with proof of purchase. (Coach House Books reserves the right to terminate the free download offer at any time.)

*This book is for my siblings and
is dedicated to our mom*

Prologue

Living with the knowledge of death is harder than it sounds. To know its scent, its swiftness, is harder still. In Toni Morrison's 1973 novel *Sula*, a melancholic WWI veteran named Shadrack takes to the streets of his small Ohio town in a sombre, one-man parade celebrating an occasion of his own invention. Clanging a cowbell and clasping a hangman's rope, Shadrack marches to pay honour to suicide – the ultimate act of taking control of one's death. Instead of allowing the spectre of his eventual end to grip him with fear, Morrison's glum soldier marks a single day in his calendar to function as an annual psychic release valve. He knows his anxieties around death are inescapable, and so he designates this day to reckon with and inhabit the gloom.

Shadrack's DIY death parade points to a trenchant truth: if you want the space to ruminate on death, dying, and loss, you've got to sanction it yourself. No one else is going to eke out room for your grief. Learning to live with loss is an uncomfortable but necessary process, yet there exists so little space to talk about death and to grapple with prolonged mourning. Even at the few 'official' moments we have carved out to directly address loss – like the funeral eulogy – there isn't much time to process, to grieve, to wallow before one is ushered toward the podium.

The eulogy is a particularly vexed art form, partly because it's a necessity, and partly because at its very heart it is an amateur's art. It is no minor footnote that most Americans fear public speaking more than death itself; the eulogy is the fraught convergence of both, combining the speaker's fear of death with that of public articulation, and layering the mess atop the experience of loss. As a consequence of our desire to distance ourselves from our fear, other matters often take precedence after a death. We have learned to push aside the emotional work of putting language to our loss. The calculations of inheritance, the listing of property, the distribution of stuff – these are the things that make up the supposedly urgent work that follows a death. Less defined, less urgent, are the muddled feelings that loss occasions: etiquette ends up taking priority over the chaos of grief. As such, the eulogy often falls flat, backsliding into clichés that have sprouted around narratives of sorrow because we are seldom granted sufficient time and emotional space to craft meaningful last words.

Some narratives of grief have found new platforms, amplifying themselves through the collective megaphone of social media. These online tributes are typically just another socially sanctioned step in an all-too-efficient grieving process, one that even acts to speed up the pace of modern mourning. Virtual eulogizing is rapidly unleashed and hashtagged, but is quickly replaced with more timely, relevant news. Suffice to say, social media mourning – beholden as it currently is to a sense of pseudo-professional productivity, and the gamified systems of likes, retweets, and shares – is not precisely a radical new way to grieve in public.

Our online lives are only part of what I'm interested in here, since the art of eulogizing has a much longer, and emotionally checkered, history. What this little book concerns itself with is the many and sundry iterations of the eulogy we find in cultural history, pop culture, literature, and philosophy, too. It turns out that whether you're an esteemed post-structuralist, a fictional widower in *Love Actually*, or Cher – you will feel like a failure in the art of eulogizing. And it's not because you didn't love fully, or even because the immensity of your grief has felled you, but because in a culture that sees death every day and yet hides the traces of grief that follow, there aren't enough words for loss.

If the elegy is a poetic form that laments its dead in verse, and the obituary announces the hard fact of loss in the newspaper – all the deaths that are fit to print – then the eulogy falls somewhere in between. Intensely personal and yet meant to be spoken aloud to other grievers, the eulogy is a ritual that overlaps with the elegy and obituary in an invisible Venn diagram of funeral rites. The eulogy is often the first chance we have to gather publicly after a death, and it's this charged moment where communities come together to puzzle over what a person meant to them when she was alive, and what she could mean now that she is dead. Does her story end in death, or is there a coda that extends even after the lights go out?

When Princess Diana died, her brother delivered a eulogy as the whole world, quite literally, watched. Buckling under the pressure of Diana's thorny kinship to the royal family, and likely under his own grief, the Earl of Spencer gave a eulogy so politically correct that it erased the flesh-and-blood woman behind the tiara. In some ways, he set the tone for how she would be remembered: as an icon that everyone wanted a piece of, but whom very few can now remember in much intimate or specific detail.

We have learned to structure our grief, however personal and inchoate, by marrying it to an invisible timeline that marches to a capitalist beat, two-stepping in time with pressures to be efficient, to progress, to – most of all – get back to work. The problem with such a regimented and overdetermined schedule is that, well, mourning doesn't work that way. There is no timeline because the work of grieving is never done. There is nothing efficient or productive about loss, but there it is all the same. Through the experience of grief, the heartbroken are uprooted from reality and planted into fantastical registers of the mind where time, results, and myths of progress don't abide. It's for this reason that, for me, grief has sometimes felt like my own personal Bermuda Triangle – an imagined place that feels very real, a vortex that has vanished my loved ones, upended reality as I've known it, and left me among the shoals to process my loss alone.

This book was written in the sombre but playful spirit of Shadrack. It is a reminder that you have to die. It is a reminder, too, that the anguish of losing is the basis of love. In the following pages I look to cinema, poetry, prose, song lyrics, and personal memory to find a bit more room for us to live with death, beyond the dictates of a calendar. I searched for eulogies that revived the dying art, because I still believe that attesting to a life – in all of its contradictions and nuance – is a confounding but loving task. Even the traumatized soldier of Morrison's *Sula* knows, despite his best attempts, that there is no outwitting loss and there is no corralling death. The reckoning is year-round.

The Fairy-Tale Funeral

Rubbing the sleep from her eyes, my mother got up very early one morning in the summer of 1981 to sit down in front of her television, the screen's artificial glow casting a welcoming cone of light toward her, to watch a fairy tale unfold. The wedding of Lady Diana Spencer to Charles, Prince of Wales, in July of that year was a spectacle par excellence – thousands of spectators lined the route of the procession through the streets of London leading to St. Paul's Cathedral, and a national holiday was declared for the occasion. My mom, Patricia, who at thirty-four was then only three years older than I am now, watched the televised event live, sitting rapt by the marriage ritual of a prince to a beautiful twenty-year-old woman plucked from much humbler beginnings. Pat was already a married mother of two (with two more, including yours truly, to arrive over the next four years), and she would soon enough be appointed to the Superior Court of Ontario as Canada's sixty-first female judge. Surely she would have been thinking about her own mother, the daughter of a British emigré who came to Canada near the dawn of the tumultuous twentieth century. Perhaps Pat made a cup of tea to underscore the moment with a tinge of colonial affinity, as she watched a softer expression of Britishness than she had known growing up. (Her mother had been rather prim, and Pat had never been a rebel – she didn't dare pierce her ears or even buy a pair of jeans until after my grandma's death.)

Diana's marriage to Charles was a PR dream for the conservative monarchy, a fairy tale that established the People's Princess as an icon of genteel white femininity. My mom was not alone in her desire to witness one young woman's transition from stylish singleton into happily ever after. Scholars have since come to agree that the ceremony, viewed by an estimated 750 million people around the globe, even revived a slumbering nostalgia for English traditions. With her kind eyes and flashing smile, Diana made the frills and pomp of the British royalty look almost trendy; she gave the family a distinctly popular celebrity they hadn't yet known in the modern era.

The nostalgia awakened by the 1981 wedding theatrics has grown into a fervour for royal Englishness that is alive and well in our own moment, from the resounding success of landed-gentry-worshipping shows like *Downton Abbey* (not to mention the serialized biopic *The Crown*) to the fastidious cataloguing of Kate Middleton's choice of pantyhose in the pages of *Vanity Fair*. I've often wondered why American publications care at all about the British royal family – the United States having been founded on the principle of independence from the Crown. I suspect that more than the alluring grace of fabled old money or a continent-sized Oedipal syndrome, the royal family is an icon of an unshakable (albeit completely oppressive) fairy-tale order. Fortified by a history of white supremacy and the colonial strength of its empire, the modern incarnation of the royal family is a site of fascination because it offers attendant fantasies of an interminable power that can never quite be revoked. A king is born by divine right, after all.

The fairy-tale order comes as succour especially to the ignorant, the anxious, and the racist elements of Western society; it is a comfortable literalization of a recognizable status quo. England's recent decision to leave the European Union (a momentous choice that tipped into reality by a margin of only 3.8 per cent) extends from the same nostalgia for a discreet fairy-tale kingdom. The vote was intended by some to settle the thorny matter of belonging: Brexit has been summed up as the shameful proof that working-class Brits voted without understanding the stakes and fell back on their inherited fears of England's invasion by foreigners. But, as the British novelist Zadie Smith put it so pithily in the *New*

York Review of Books, 'a referendum turns out to be a very ineffective hammer for a thousand crooked nails,' and the Brexit results were a failure. 'The notable feature of neoliberalism is that it feels like you can do nothing to change it,' Smith explains, 'but this vote offered up the rare prize of causing a chaotic rupture in a system that more usually steamrolls all in its path.' Brexit, the framing of which appealed to an imaginary, even fairy-tale-like, historical era and completely ignored the contentious relationships within the U.K. between England and Scotland or Northern Ireland, was brought to pass by a wild act of solipsism, one that stomped its foot in reaction to a global idea of belonging at the cost of the hard-won idea of Great Britain.

The 'deep fracture in British society that has been thirty years in the making' described by Smith brings us back to Diana, and to the ways her image was manipulated around themes of kinship, upward mobility, and fairy-tale comfort, associations she eventually came to chafe against following her marriage into the royal family. Thirty years prior to Brexit, Princess Diana's down-to-earth charms were fraying the edges of class boundaries, even as her story seemed to lend credence to the Cinderella fairy tale of marrying above one's class. Sixteen years after Diana's wedding, I slumped out of bed at 4 a.m. to watch a televised spectacle with an even larger global audience: her funeral.

The optics between the two events were similar: both involved a seemingly interminable procession, the streets lined with cut flowers laid like little Queen's Guards wrapped in plastic, hours of live coverage, and never-ending montages of Diana's face. According to British sociologist John Urry, two billion people tuned in to watch as the princess was laid to rest. Diana's brother, Charles, 9th Earl of Spencer, gave the official eulogy, a somewhat confused affair. He lauded the late princess as a 'very British girl' but also as one 'who transcended nationality.' To the Earl of Spencer, Diana was able to emanate beyond the borders of England, expanding her charitable empire, without, for all that, losing a drop of her Englishness. It's as apt a synopsis of Britain's colonial mindset as you could ask for. He reminded the assembled mourners that Diana was 'someone with a natural nobility' who nonetheless 'was classless.' Muddled by grief, certainly, it would seem the earl's speech was shaped also by a deep misunderstanding of both his sister and what a thoughtful and honest eulogy can do.

By the time I was tuning in to that fateful afternoon procession in London, my mom's marriage had, like Diana's, unravelled and I was spending the night at my dad's condo. Across town, my mom was likewise crawling out of bed to watch teary-eyed as Diana's funeral cortege proceeded from Kensington Palace to Westminster Abbey. I remember thinking the occasion so important that I decided to record the multi-hour event on VHS – as though the tape would be my teenaged way of bearing witness to Diana's death, a cheap but sincere relic of loss. I watched the funeral because my mom was watching the funeral, and my mom watched because if her mom had been alive she would have watched, too. It was unlike anything I had ever seen before. Death in my family, and in all the families I had observed in my young life, was dealt with modestly, swiftly, and without talk of it later.

There is a tendency in Western culture to avoid dwelling for too long on the realities of death. Death is uncomfortable, and as such we tend to simply ignore, to the best of our abilities, the most complicated feelings of grief that come with it. Watching Diana's funeral procession was the first time I found myself encountering the event of death. Nine years later, my mom would take her last breath – a raspy, hollow quake – in the oncology wing of St. Joseph's hospital in Hamilton, Ontario. Shortly after, I would think back to Diana's funeral and wonder how the public mourning of the People's Princess was the most prominent model for the experience of loss available to me, a map that could never match the new and unfamiliar territory of my life with grief.

Critical theorist Sara Ahmed has written lucidly about the tendency prevalent in Britain and North America to deny bad feelings and to champion the 'good' ones. That is, to make difficult or bad feelings, like despair, more productive or useful (for example, donating money to a memorial fund in the name of an incredibly wealthy figure because you don't know how else to express your heartache). Ahmed writes in *The Promise of Happiness* that as a culture we are addicted to happiness to the extent that any emotion that doesn't contribute to utter contentment must be quelled. This is not only to protect you from staying too long in the doldrums, but also to prevent your negativity, sadness, or shame from impinging on other people's pursuit of 'the good life.' This need to be happy for yourself and for others morphs into a demand, an injunction to buck up and smile because *life's too short, carpe diem, you only live once*, etc.

Ahmed deflates this grandiloquent narrative of self-actualization and self-help, underscoring the myriad ways that a society based on free-market principles is also one that regulates for a baseline level of contentment. She aims to disabuse us of the notion that the social regulation of bad feelings is in the service of our collective happiness. Rather, we are systematically encouraged to repress loss and grief as a way of maintaining productivity for the benefit of a capitalist system. Minimizing any form of dissatisfaction – even when, for instance, that dissatisfaction is entirely warranted by the death of a loved one – is a socially enforced strategy of our neo-liberal era.

This insistence on persistent happiness also works to make invisible certain kinds of emotional labour. Ahmed takes the American housewife as a prime example of this positivity ideology at work: the happy housewife of 1950s America was depicted in television, in film, in newspapers and magazines as a woman who found extreme pleasure and satisfaction in tirelessly working (without pay) to keep her house, children, and husband in order. Following in the footsteps of Betty Friedan and *The Feminine Mystique*, Ahmed illustrates how 'the happy housewife is a fantasy figure that erases the signs of labour under the sign of happiness.' Under happiness, all manner of patriarchal bullshit is forgiven.

In part, the desire to hide inequality beneath the banner of happiness is your run-of-the-mill hegemonic ploy, but it also makes it seem as though any negative feeling is unhealthy, abnormal, and annoying. Expressing grief in a culture that urges happiness becomes almost unimaginable in any sustained or thoughtful way. And that's where you find the guts of Ahmed's argument: being angry, or being sad or grief-stricken, is not a character flaw. A false dichotomy has taken root around our notion of happiness wherein anything that does not contribute to that happiness is the enemy. The result of this cult relationship to being happy is that maintaining contentment requires a relinquishing of death and any and all difficult feelings.

In similar terms voiced stateside, Barbara Ehrenreich argues that Americans are relentlessly positive people, obsessed by an optimism so sunny it is often blinding. Consequently, they find it incredibly difficult to express grief, to feel loss, without immediately displacing it. In *Bright-Sided: How Positive Thinking Is Undermining America*, Ehrenreich argues that this national attitude of unwarranted optimism has snuggled up to another of the country's foundational myths: that of the extreme benefits of industrial, then consumer, capitalism for all. Ehrenreich writes that 'the consumer culture encourages individuals to want more – cars, larger homes, television sets, cell phones, gadgets of all kinds – and positive thinking is ready at hand to tell them they deserve more and can have it if they really want it and are willing to make the effort to get it.' Late capitalism feeds on positive thinking, and positive thinking feasts right back. Positive thinking 'requires deliberate self-deception, including a constant effort to repress or block out unpleasant possibilities and "negative" thoughts' – the same can be said of our current economic system, a system that creates unimaginable wealth disparity.

Campy and flamboyant, Sir Elton John, a close friend of Diana's, gave the people's eulogy for the People's Princess. The straining piano tribute 'Candle in the Wind' famously commemorated the fallen princess in song. What is remarkable about 'Candle in the Wind' is not its saccharine lyrics or schmaltzy melody – in this regard, it is a pedestrian example of An Elton John Song. The song wasn't even an original: John reworded and rerecorded his 1973 ballad of the same name, which he had originally written to eulogize Marilyn Monroe. Swapping 'Norma Jeane' for 'English Rose' in his reprise for Princess Di, he pretty much called it a day's work. What *is* remarkable about John's eulogy song is how its outpouring of unabashed chintz allowed a nation of stiff upper lips to get weepy.

As the Earl of Spencer's eulogy sketches in its convoluted terms, Diana had become a fraught icon in Britain's cultural imagination by the time of her death. She had, as media scholar Raka Shome puts it, 'significantly disturbed the racial and patriarchal bounds of Englishness.' First with her extreme candour in a BBC interview about the royal family, then through her post-royal relationships with the Muslim Pakistani doctor Hasnat Khan and, finally, Dodi Fayed – whose wildly wealthy family of Egyptian descent had, despite owning and operating the British landmark department store Harrods, never been granted English citizenship – Diana had migrated from the accepted image of a lily-white fairy-tale princess to that of a wanton woman eager to embrace the foreign other. Shome explains that Diana, having stumbled off her pedestal as white feminine icon, became the visual instantiation of the 'identity crisis' that had struck the country in the late 1990s. In her death, Diana became the screen onto which Britain's royal subjects might project their anxieties regarding that crisis. During the final decade of the twentieth century, the U.K. had succeeded home rule to Scotland, had relinquished hold of Hong Kong, its last colony; England had seen the Conservatives ousted from parliament after a long eighteen years, and had watched as support for the monarchy waned and the public balked at the royal family's string of divorces and public mishaps.

Almost immediately following Diana's death in France, the royal family was criticized across various media outlets for appearing unmoved by their loss. They followed royal protocol and grieving rites, like attending church the morning after the crash, which appeared to many as proof of a love of tradition over a love of Diana. The two aren't mutually exclusive, but the contrast between the staid and contained expression of royal grief and the effusive public mourning seemed stark. These adherences to tradition would not, of course, likely come as a surprise to Diana herself: she had been cruelly and often publicly versed in the cool rigidity with which the family operates. Always a square peg in the round hole of the monarchy, Diana, it is often said, was never a good fit; she had flair where the family wanted reserve, she was outspoken where they wanted tight-lipped, and she loved a husband who had always loved someone else.

Once Diana finally achieved some happiness of her own, apart from the family, she could openly deviate from the scripted behaviour befitting a royal – to be demure, quiet, devoted, beige. She emerged back into the world after her divorce, having shown the fairy tale defunct. In fact, to the chagrin of the family, she hardly seemed to miss her seat at the royal table at all. Her new life, adventurous and romantic, recast her image in a very different light from the one that had first brought her into the public eye. At the end of her life, this 'very British girl' loved a man totally unlike Charles (the *most* British man). Fayed had found his success in business, was reportedly given to demonstrating and celebrating romance, and was neither white nor a British citizen. To the British public, it was as if the narrative of their love called into doubt Diana's 'very' Britishness (defined narrowly and hegemonically in line with an old imperial order). Then came 'Candle in the Wind,' which re-codified Diana as an English rose – an archaic, imperial image that had been tarnished by her tabloid-exploited relationship with Fayed.

John vowed to never perform his eulogy song ever again, a gesture meant to mimic the transience of his unlasting friend. Refusing to perform 'Candle in the Wind' also functioned to make the song seem all the more precious – at least in its Diana-not-Marilyn version – and it worked. John has sung the 1973 ballad many times over, though never its 1997 redux, but he did press a single of his Diana tribute. The 1997 'Candle in the Wind' was released in September of that year and sold a record-breaking 33 million copies worldwide. In the U.K. it became the country's best-selling single of all time and came close to that in the U.S., too. It also won John a Grammy. John treated his Diana tribute single like a rare commodity, but a commodity nonetheless, and its one live performance gave its expansive distribution a sense of scarcity that didn't actually exist.

Let's revisit John's choice to reprise his original tribute to Monroe on the occasion of his once-royal friend's death. If nothing else, a eulogy is meant to be unique. Heartfelt. Singular. Even though death comes for us all, the way in which the final moment happens is totally unique for everyone. No two deaths are the same. The contemporary eulogy is meant to address this to a small public for whom the specificity of a given loss is shared. In the instance of 'Candle in the Wind,' there was a lot more emphasis put on *what* John's audience had lost: an image of charity, an icon of motherhood, a portrait of femininity. Diana the flesh-and-blood woman was missing from this tribute and was delivered a kind of second death in the song's hook. John turned the princess to wax, morphing her into equal parts Icarus and Eric Clapton's eternal flame. Despite Diana's work with world leaders to eradicate AIDS, despite her having raised two children and gotten out from beneath her manipulative husband, despite being a beloved international figure espousing peace and gay rights, John likened her to a measly candle on a drafty day.

A eulogy is an offering. It's an attempt to provide some comfort as the first spoken words after a death. To be sure, that's a tall order. To sum up the significance of a life in a short speech? It is impossible, and even to attempt that summing up, that siphoning off, feels inadequate. There is certainly an unsettling crassness to it. In this way, the eulogy can easily become a vehicle for cliché: if we can't find the right words at the right time, at least we can find some safe, well-worn ones to fill the space. And that's exactly what John did with 'Candle in the Wind.' Maybe, especially given his grief, we could forgive John for being lazy. Yet, there's something more disturbing at play here. In choosing to revamp his ode to Monroe for Diana, John drew an analogy between the two women that cheapens the death of each. The 1997 iteration of the song flattens Diana's life, painting her as yet another tragic blond bombshell.

It could be said that John revised 'Candle in the Wind' as a way of castigating the paparazzi for their central role in Diana's death in the Pont de l'Alma tunnel. One might then catch the resemblance to the unrelenting Hollywood gossip rags that hounded Monroe until she took her own life. But what's the point of forging this fatalistic solidarity between the two women? By linking the deaths of the Princess and Munroe, John revealed a few things. First, his lack of imagination. Second, when it comes to popular female icons, people prefer to stick to clear-cut and recognizable tropes. And third, with 'Candle in the Wind,' John chose to keep Diana in the realm of image as opposed to flesh. Diana's face, name, and story were so often collapsed into grainy photos that had the power to make people buy magazines. But celebrating this particular quality of her being dissociates her from the life she led behind those photos, and in sensationalizing her glamorous image in his tribute, John tacitly condones the same spirit that led to the paparazzi chasing her at 120 kilometres per hour through a Paris tunnel. In fact, the lyrics suggest John hoped his friend, tormented so by the press, would be able to find not only peace, but a sliver of happiness, in her eternal rest. 'Candle in the Wind' makes it seem as though – *even after you die* – happiness remains the ultimate goal.

John wasn't the only one holding fast to cliché to aid in mourning Diana. England's grieving public took over established monuments in Paris and London when Diana died, creating spontaneous memorials. The cellophane-wrapped outpouring of flowers at the gates of Kensington Palace came to be known as Diana's 'floral revolution' – an odd designation that calls to mind the distinctly American flower-power revolution of the 1960s, yet with the word *floral* lending the phrase a buttoned-up British tinge. In Paris, a monument marking the relationship between America and France – a scale replica of the Statue of Liberty's torch called the Flamme de la Liberté that sits near the Place de l'Alma – became a site-specific and unofficial memorial to Diana and Fayed. There was a tendency in the wake of Diana's death to search for sites already loaded with meaning and to mourn her there – to layer her death atop other established histories. That is, to grieve her in cliché.

This isn't so odd, this reappropriation of monuments in Diana's name, except that when it came time to build a dedicated memorial, it seems as though no one could come up with anything very good. Australian architecture scholar Nicole Sully notes that the permanent monuments built in Diana's memory have been, like the Earl of Spencer's eulogy, confused. There is a neglected, hard-to-find garden in Paris nowhere near the scene of the accident; an eleven-kilometre walkway through London that mostly covers royal grounds; a Peter Pan–themed playground near Kensington Palace; and a peculiarly modernist fountain in Hyde Park that has proven too expensive to keep up and has come to be known colloquially as Diana's Ditch. Sully writes that 'substitution and appropriation have proved a persistent theme in the commemoration of Diana, Princess of Wales.' In other words, no one knew who Diana really was, so they pasted her image onto other recognizable images that already held meaning and cultural value. This cut-and-paste approach to mourning Diana is precisely what John did with his eulogy. He couldn't come up with anything original to say about the princess, so he overlaid her tragedy onto an equally sensational one.

There is, however, at least one endearing act of Diana commemoration I can think of, affecting for both its quirkiness and its figurative shrug of the shoulders toward tradition. This act comes in the form of fiction, through the character of the beloved spinster Bridget Jones. In the novel by Helen Fielding, Bridget documents hearing and absorbing the news of Diana's death in a couple of the short, often pronounless entries in her diary. She considers going down to the growing memorial outside of Kensington Palace and decides to go; considers buying flowers from 'the petrol station,' then learns they have sold out. In the end, Bridget buys a copy of *Vogue* for Diana and leaves it hidden under the more 'respectable' choice of flowers that others have left. Bridget's rationale is that the magazine is 'not perfect but everyone will have brought flowers and know she liked *Vogue*.' Though she feels embarrassed going alone down to the mourning crowds, she realizes that 'when think about it Princess Diana was often on own.' Bridget thinks of Diana at 2 a.m.: 'really she was the patron saint of Singleton women because she started off like the archetypal fairy tale doing what we all thought we were supposed to do i.e. marry a handsome Prince and she was honest enough to say that life is not like that.' Maybe this fictive account of one woman's gesture isn't much, but at least this small act takes into account Diana's own interests. It is only a glossy consumer product that Bridget leaves at the gates of the palace, but it is – along with her loneliness – representative of something she shared with the princess.

Bridget is not inured to the frenzied public grieving for Diana, but, amid the collective surge of emotion, she takes a moment to distinguish the woman who is gone from the image of her that will live on. The Bridget Jones books are an interesting set of popular-culture artifacts, getting as they do into the details of loneliness, melancholy, and the self-improvement treadmill many find themselves so easily trapped on. It is a story of when the road to self-actualization can go awry but also of how it can right itself after failure – Bridget Jones is neither perfectly happy nor a morose lost cause.

Alas, despite this original – and refreshing – portrait of a woman living relatively easily with the complexities of human emotion, refusing to flatten them into camps of happy or sad, 2016's film adaptation of the series purposely ignores Fielding's nuance. In the third book of the series, Mark Darcy has died and Bridget is alone once again, struggling to figure out online dating while also managing single motherhood. The movie cuts out the death part, replacing it with a love triangle.

Despite how comforting it may be to witness different models for how one might grieve in the modern world – especially from a character as lovable and fallible as Bridget – death is once again sidestepped in favour of lightheartedness.

I'm sympathetic to our human tendency to fall into cliché when it comes to commemoration, in part because we are creatures of procrastination, and we seek safety and well-worn comforts in lots of ways; these aren't vices, they're mechanisms. Yet, I also find it important to resist some of those tendencies – especially our capacity to repress and push away hard feelings – when it comes to a moment as significant as death. The eulogy captures its subject in an uncomfortable double bind wherein she is forced to rush her grieving for the sake of articulateness. This puts an unfathomable weight on the eulogy that ironically may lead the speaker to make the eulogy lighter, less thoughtful, more dependent on well-known but meaningless tropes and empty phrases.

The proceeds from Elton John's song went not into his coffers but into a temporary memorial fund in Diana's name – a fund that hundreds of thousands of people donated to. Unsure of what to do with their sad feelings, they took solace in converting those emotions – *So hard to process! So tiring to feel!* – into money. Not incidentally, the first official act of commemoration for Diana was a £5 sterling coin with her image emblazoned on it in 1999. Money talks when we prefer not to. This preference to pay out instead of process is likely also the reason there is pressure to quickly return to work after a death. Time for bereavement is short, if it comes at all, and productivity is a way of opting out of the slow, painstaking processing of grief. Being absorbed in your grief does not hold any social value, in part because being unproductive is counterintuitive under capitalism: we derive value from the production, circulation, and distribution of capital goods or services, and maximum output means maximum value. The griever's absorption might be framed in terms of narcissism or laziness or navel-gazing, but the cardinal sin of our current economic system is the expression of apathy toward the production of wealth.

When the news broke that David Robert Jones, known to most as Bowie, had died on January 10, 2016, Twitter erupted with links to the performer's greatest hits, GIFs of his stellar onscreen performances, and photo stills of his long career as an androgynous heartthrob. Bowie's son, Duncan Jones, announced his father's death in a tweet of just eighty characters: 'Very sorry and sad to say it's true. I'll be offline for a while. Love to all.' Nearly 100,000 people liked his tweet. It was retweeted 66,549 times. While Jones carved out an indeterminate segment of time to grieve in private, public mourning immediately took centre stage. Celebrities began to disseminate bite-sized condolences and the general public liked and shared them as though in virtual kinship with the stars. Mark Ruffalo tweeted, 'Rip Father of all us freaks,' while Elijah Wood, feeling a touch of *poiesis*, wrote, 'Never imagined a world without him. He has ascended into the cosmos from whence he came. Farewell, David Bowie.' A-, B-, and C-listers publicly marked their sense of loss in what resembled a game of grief-stricken one-upmanship. Maintaining a fidelity to the language of the internet, where these messages were being posted, Russell Crowe capped his tweet off with a searchable '#sorrow.' Likewise, Trevor Moran shared his shock in a tweet that married form with content; it read: 'Omg RIP David Bowie :(.' The inundation of images and condolences continued with no direct addressee. These micro-eulogies were intended for everyone who might read them, but the very contingency of that audience – *who would be reading? how many people? would they retweet and share?* – renders its members merely hypothetical; in the end, these missives were meant for no one. Amid the effort to say something universal through social media – i.e., 'The world is sad Bowie died' – the death of David Jones was leached of its particularity. The tenor of many of these tiny eulogies was so declaratively universal that they rang hollow: heard by everyone and no one.

When Prince died a short four months after Bowie, 2016 was declared a writeoff on these same social media platforms: no good could come from a year that had seen death claim not one but two beloved members of music royalty (Leonard Cohen would also die later that year, among other losses to have stained 2016). Continuing to hyperlink to Prince's Twitter account by using his handle – @Prince – and hashtagging his name, fans and adoring celebrities kept his social media presence alive while his body was being autopsied. A series of thank-yous peppered celebrity tweets, and in this way, Prince's virtual presence continued to be addressed as though he might be able to intercept the messages. Feeling clever, Sarah Michelle Gellar wrote, 'This is what it sounds like #whendovescry #rip #Prince,' while Cara Delevingne preferred a simple, reality-denying hashtag: '#PRINCEWILLNEVERDIE.'

Twitter is an imperfect tool for communicating, and the surface-level interactions that it trades in can distract from the possibility of those interactions having any depth. That so many of the celebrity tweets meant to memorialize Bowie and Prince were tacky does not mean they were devoid of sincerity. The risk of heralding these micro-eulogies as the 'new way we grieve' in the era of social media is to make grief itself a fetish object: something to be fawned over, held up and examined, and then put behind glass and forgotten. The phenomenon of grief, like that of celebrity, becomes in this fetishistic mode depersonalized, remote rather than intimate.

To borrow a question from theorist Anne A. Cheng, what do the politics of performance and celebrity 'mean for someone seen at once too much and not at all?' Everyone knew Bowie, but few knew David Jones; everyone knew Prince, but who were the intimates of Prince Rogers Nelson? It is only fitting that tributes to these icons would encompass this split between a glamorous celebrity visibility and a certain individual invisibility. Both performers presented the self as a function of art and, likewise, as a commodity; in grieving each of these particular artists, we invariably reckon with the imbrications of artistic and commercial value.

Prince and Bowie, equally bewitching in the ways they played with gender and expression, were decade-spanning musicians who carved out a queer way of being in a straight world. From the ground up, Prince shifted the terms of masculinity. As Vanessa Friedman wrote in the *New York Times* shortly after his death, 'The high heel was the through-line of his wardrobe for the four decades he was in the public eye, the consistent base upon which he layered all sorts of style and character changes. Prince wore heels when he barely wore anything at all (just bikini bottoms and a trench coat); he wore them in "Purple Rain" and with baroque brocade; he paired them with pastel suits, laser-cut, bottom-baring jumpsuits'; the list goes on. Bowie, too, shirked the sartorial cage of gendered dress and proudly donned bodysuits, dresses, leotards, and reams of silk. Fluid conceptions of sex, fashion, and desire informed both artists and cascaded naturally into their music, with lyrics that embraced an unconventional but welcomed capaciousness. Heeding Bowie's call to 'turn and face the strange,' fans relaxed into queerer, less conventionally defined versions of themselves.

Both men gave 'strange' a good name, which endeared them to many outcasts, rebels, and romantics. But the strangeness of Bowie's angular mystique and Prince's knowing smirk, the novelty of their androgynous moving bodies, also functioned to make them seem immortal. They were such iconic oddballs that the public expressed shock at the news of their respective deaths, as though their enchanting antinormativity ought to have acted as a shield or form of cover from mortality. The repeated articulation of shock and surprise and disbelief and denial is a telling obfuscation of death. Neither man could be considered old, and yet it wasn't the age they died that appeared to baffle fans, it was that as icons they were never meant to be fallible, to be weak, to be human.

Twitter allows for a user to become an instant eulogizer, to step up to the virtual podium and speak to a public on the occasion of loss. Yet, it's not the content of what people say that irks so much as the competitive edge to it – the metrics upon which Twitter and other social media platforms are built gamify all of our interactions, including acts of mourning. These metrics make grief something calculable, divisible into categories and columns, reducible when it's not. Expressing grief on a platform like Twitter – where each act of expression can be measured according to an objective set of engagement analytics to be amassed, collected, counted, and monitored – is bound to affect its pitch. Not all gestures of grief on social media are inherently devoid of significance, and yet there's something about the norms and customs of grieving on these platforms that stacks the deck against deeper reflection. In the wake of Bowie's death, then Prince's, the tidy online frenzy of micro-eulogies appeared briefly before users moved on to other things – as though the work of grieving could be so thoroughly routinized, compact, and easy to dispense with.

Megan Quinn, a Toronto grief worker and counsellor, says she is able to find a silver lining in the fact that people are talking about grief in at least some capacity: 'I'm just happy and grateful to see any conversation about grief, because we often deny it. We're so good at denying grief and the process.' She likens the quick pace of online grieving to what she sees around her every day. 'I think we move from grief quickly anyway – so we are just seeing it online in that same format. That's what I see in interpersonal interactions anyway. At the news of the death, at the funeral, for a few weeks after, you can shout your grief from the rooftops, you can cry and that's fine,' she says, 'but after a couple weeks, it's uncomfortable for others, and you are expected to stop. Those are the messages we send, so perhaps it's being demonstrated online because that's how we deal with grief as a larger society.' There's already too brief a window in which to grieve, but now we are seeing – through the glass of social media – just how compressed that time frame really is.

Quinn describes this anxious tendency within our culture to relegate grief to its dark corners, out of the way, where it can be more easily forgotten. She explains that at the end of the day, grief is just too awkward for those untouched by it. 'I think until you come to grief, it's really hard to understand fully,' says Quinn. 'It's really hard to intimately relate to that kind of pain, that kind of darkness, if you haven't been there yourself. The folks that haven't come to grief – bless them, they're only doing the best they can – they're just situating the social discourse that they think is right, and that we have set up, but they are the ones who are silencing the people that really need to talk about their grief, their loss, and what's going on.' The problem, she suggests, is that the people who don't know grief are so put off by open acts of mourning that there is a sense of a social limit on the ways the grief-stricken can describe and live with their pain. ' If the grief is not yours,' Quinn says, 'it's uncomfortable.'

The expectation that a mourner in the first flush of grief should be able to synthesize a person's character into a pint-sized public speech is, frankly, a big ask. And why must it be done in front of everybody? What benefit is there to wrenching individuals from their private acts of mourning into a room where their dearly departed is rhetorically catalogued and broken down into component parts? For that matter, who is the eulogy really for? Is it for the living, we who may require some words of comfort, or is it for the dead? Is the eulogy made up of phrases the speaker hopes might fall on spectral ears?

Joan Didion's mourning memoir, *The Year of Magical Thinking*, brims with truisms for the bereaved. 'Grief turns out to be a place none of us know until we reach it,' for example, or 'Grief has no distance. Grief comes in waves, paroxysms, sudden apprehensions that weaken the knees and blind the eyes and obliterate the dailiness of life' – when grief comes, equilibrium goes. Didion's claim that grief can set the mind into a tailspin of fantastical thinking, where the mourner's ability to think rationally falls out of the picture for a while, feels true. The profound intimacy of loss can reorder the way a person relates to the world, collapsing the distance between the experience of the physical, rational world and that of internal experience, rendering that distance meaningless. In this Didion-inflected way, we might conceive of the eulogy as a kind of incantation to the dead – meant *really* for them. And yet, we eulogize for an audience, for those of us who are left behind. Grief, after all, afflicts only the living.

The eulogy is as much about marking the loss suffered by a community as it is about addressing one's own pain: at the intersection between the public and private, the eulogy performs some heavy work. While it may feel that the right time to say goodbye never arrives, the brief interlude between the death of a loved one and the eulogy's performance requires a lot of compression – so much processing of loss needs to happen so quickly. In addition to this necessary swiftness comes the pressure to make sense of a private life as it relates to a broader collective. The eulogy is meant to give closure to a group of mourners, and also to reflect on the end of the deceased's association with the assembled group. This is true equally on a scale as intimate as the nuclear family and as broad as a nation. And so the eulogy functions as a kind of border control, tallying who still belongs and whose membership has expired.

Sometimes this looks like the reclaiming of citizenship ties that may have frayed over time. Recall, for example, the British public's jumping at the chance to 'reclaim' Princess Diana from her international infamy. The opposite is also possible: the citizenship of the dead may be called into question, revoked as a matter of ideology if not paperwork. Consider Tamerlan Tsarnaev, who, with his brother Dzhokhar, bombed the Boston Marathon in 2013. Tamerlan was fatally shot by the police during his apprehension, and in the ensuing coverage his American citizenship was near-universally downplayed across media outlets, while his Chechen background and early childhood in Kyrgyzstan and Russia were emphasized. Dzhokhar has since been sentenced to death by lethal injection on federal charges – he is the living dead. To underscore the foreignness of the Tsarnaev brothers serves as one last chance to declare them un-American and to reject any national affiliation to them. The eulogy speaks to the values of the loudest group of assembled mourners, naturally. Eulogy and legacy go hand in hand, and writing the one means casting the other in ink, too.

I tend to think Sophocles's rabble-rousing Antigone, who questioned the sharp divide between private and public grieving, got the connection between citizenship and grief as close to right as anyone ever will. In the fifth-century-BCE play, Antigone's power-hungry uncle decrees that her brother Polyneices won't get proper burial rites because he is seen as a traitor to the Oedipal family nation-state. Antigone marches out into the desert to bury her brother anyway. Vultures circle the dead from above while guards snitch on Antigone, but her grief proves stronger than her obedience. She doesn't need the rest of the community to honour Polyneices, but she will be damned if she doesn't mourn him properly herself.

After my first reading of Sophocles's play, I sat in awe of Antigone's unbridled anger and her unwavering conviction that she would take up whatever space necessary to mourn, and to mourn selfishly, without community, without an audience. I had been carrying a mental image of a Victorian lady beating her chest and sobbing in a garish performance of sorrow as my sole example of being devastated, grief-stricken. The image didn't match up with my own experience of loss. I didn't want to weep at my mother's funeral, where I felt scrutinized, on display for the audience. My grief felt too intimate, but I also felt an awareness that the stone-cold face I donned was too crass, too unfeeling, for this woman I had known like a second heartbeat. Then I read *Antigone*, and I felt the chord she struck between righteous anger and total devotion to the dead reverberate in me. I wanted to keep burying my mom forever like Antigone kept burying her brother. I didn't want my 'work' of mourning to ever be complete. If I had been able to cross the boundaries of centuries and fiction, I like to think Antigone would have grabbed me sternly by my shoulders with dirt still beneath her nails and said, 'Julia, you are going to be sad forever.' It would have been a relief.

But Antigone chose another course for herself. Instead of staying sad forever, she decided on total annihilation. She hanged herself with the veil intended for her wedding, permanently opting out of all future rituals. Some say Antigone died because she couldn't live without Polyneices – but that's only one theory among many, and Antigone herself never gives a straight answer. I tend to think it wasn't the grief that led her to kill herself, but rather the stifling conventions that ensured there would be no space for that grief anywhere in social life. Dying yourself doesn't resurrect the dead, and loving means loving even in absence, I think.

Much ink has been spilled on why Antigone risked and ultimately took her own life to grieve her brother – she's morphed into an intellectual diamond polished for decades by philosophers and literary theorists alike. But what I want to distill from Antigone's story is not why she did it, but why there's been this need to mark limits around private grieving and to make certain sanctioned forms of it public-facing. To deny Polyneices his right to be mourned was for his sister as catastrophic as his death. To expel his remains from Thebes and leave him unburied was a brutal act of dehumanization that made him literal bird meat.

Ritual is more than mere etiquette – there is a sanctity to ritual that can offer comfort, structure, and affirmation. As theorist Julia Kristeva puts it, we as humans have this innate, primordial, and 'incredible need to believe' in something larger than ourselves. Born into the world without language or understanding, we piece together our small patch of the universe bit by bit. Even as we eventually acquire language and accumulate knowledge, the world remains in large degree overwhelming to us. Rituals are a way of formalizing our incredible need to believe that there is more to our existence than chaos. Funeral rites can bring sincere comfort when, in our loss and disorientation, we frankly don't know what to do with ourselves. But they can also be restrictive – too proper – and worse, a way of performing a kind of grief that enables us to avoid experiencing our grief in full.

I wonder if there is a way we might pay homage to the disorientation that loss brings and leave some room to not know what to do in the face of it. Carving out the space to not have any answers, to be confounded by your loss, would mean taking stock of the fact that the world, as you've known it, is different now. That's what drew me to Antigone – it wasn't her suicidal end, but rather the alcove of grief she created for herself in order to feel like total, unintelligible shit. What space is there in this world for every mourner to do the same, if she needs?

Traditionally, funeral orations – public displays in honour of the dead, and the original eulogies – were performed only for important men: politicians, men of letters, and the like.

The most famous of these is the funeral oration that Pericles gave at the end of the Peloponnesian War to commemorate all of the soldiers who died in battle. His speech was plainly about citizenship and the men who fought to protect it. I suppose there was no need at the time to pretend that death was individualized; when you live and die first and foremost as a soldier, your death has already been given a value as it relates to your sovereign. Serving a leader or nation-state was not a choice, and so living a long, full life was never on the proverbial table. To individualize a death, like that of Polyneices's, is to give the middle finger to the adamantly collective notion of citizenship. You lived, served, and died for the pleasure and protection of the nation, and you were memorialized collectively for your service.

The history of the eulogy, then, is a history of power. Chaucer's saucy Wife of Bath puts it another way in her speech on misogyny in *The Canterbury Tales*, while looking at an oil painting depicting the animal kingdom with a proud lion at its centre. In what is clearly an allegory for patriarchal power, the Wife of Bath asks, 'tell me who painted the lion, tell me who?' In short, she asks a question of history. Who chronicles victory? Put slightly differently, the Wife of Bath underlines for us that the lion (and the alpha dominance it stands for) isn't the whole picture, but it's the part of the scene, of history, that gets painted. She is often read as a lascivious husband-hunter (which she is), but she is also a great strategist and a sharp thinker who wouldn't be eulogized like her male peers. The eulogies we have recorded in history are those of 'distinguished' individuals who wielded power in a straightforward way.

We claim the dead to buttress our notion of a public if and when those dead reflect how that public likes to be represented. The eulogy is a point at which we enable the deceased to mirror and affirm social values one more time. Because mourning publicly becomes an act of identification, the micro-eulogies we deliver online become extensions of our personas. Celebrity deaths reveal the unbearable fact that no one is impervious, no one is immortal – not even those, like Prince and Bowie, whose impact on the culture makes them appear to be not quite of this world. The confrontation with finitude – this reminder of the limits of our being – is not a plot twist. As supernatural as Prince might have seemed amid the vibrations of a particularly virtuosic guitar riff, his death was always as guaranteed to him as ours is to us.

Prince was much too young, only fifty-seven when he died of an accidental opioid overdose, but the promise of a long life is a modern invention. Much like the American conceit of 'the good life' (brimming with autonomy, upward mobility, and wealth, among other things), the promise of longevity is not just a fantasy but a death-denying delusion. The image of the old lady in her nightie, lying on her deathbed surrounded by loved ones, wistfully drifting off into the next world, is not how it will go for most of us, and, more insidiously, it suggests we have some power to curate our deaths when the time inevitably comes. We have modern medicine to thank for the lengthening of the average North American life, but with those scientific medians comes the notion that we are guaranteed a longer life span, owed one even, because it is now a statistical possibility. While I'm grateful for the antibiotics that rid me of the scarlet fever I contracted in the third grade, there's no guarantee I will see an overripe old age – science can only predict and protect so far. Thinking that we can shape and choose how we will die is simple hubris, a condition from which we may at any moment be utterly cured: cancer can grow undetected past the point of no return before showing up on a scan, a train can malfunction, an aneurysm can burst, depression can overwhelm. Death is certain, but its circumstances are often unpredictable.

What would it mean to live in the knowledge of death without that knowledge warping into terror? Not to follow the platitudinous call to 'live every day as though it were your last,' but to maybe live as though death were not antithetical to life. Death is what gives that life its impetus, its very breath.

On the surface, talking about loss collectively through social media perhaps ought to be seen as a good thing. Bringing grief into the foreground of the cultural landscape might be seen as an antidote to the greater and more prevalent tendency to avoid addressing death directly. Letting others share in your grief can be viewed as a step toward recognizing how integral loss is to life. With the pressures to remain eternally optimistic that bombard us on a daily basis, it might seem as though carving out a little time to be blue together – even if only virtually – is a small act of civil disobedience. And this feeling of disobedience (a small rush, a tiny comfort) might be especially significant for those who reached out to their online communities and strangers alike with personal anecdotes of feeling queer and closeted until the likes of Bowie, space alien and lover, came along and shed a little light into those shadows. Or, likewise, the lonely hearts who wrote about the ways in which Prince – a black, gender-warping man from Mormon Minneapolis – recast for them what it meant to be in one's own body and to find some bliss: 'legit changed my life hearing prince say "im not a woman. im not a man. im something you will never understand,"' wrote one Twitter user, @fijiwatergod, while another, @yung_nitsua, reflected that 'Prince was the first person who made me feel like it was maybe possibly ok to stand in my masculinity a little differently.' Comedian Aparna Nancherla gestured to Prince's otherworldliness without slipping into the more common death-denying narrative that prevailed online: 'I think we all knew Prince would leave the party before it got lame, even if it was his party.'

When an icon like Bowie or Prince dies, there is a rush on Facebook, Twitter, Instagram, to be the first to announce it. Without taking a moment to think of the life extinguished, users post and retweet the news of a celebrity death as though beating others to it means tapping into a virgin trove of social capital. Twitter and Facebook profit off our engagement on their platforms – that is the exact premise of their business – and they do so best when that engagement is at its shallowest. When death starts trending, we witness information capitalism in action. And so it was that an adoring and voracious public eulogized these men online and off: through candid fan interviews airing as part of twenty-four-hour news coverage of their deaths, to streetside memorials, to the retweeting of other musicians' pithy goodbyes, to film-screening tributes, and more. Lyrics were shared, memes created – the internet gave way, if for just a short while, to tenderness. But it also did what it does best, giving us the tools to measure and compete in our tendernesses. Who was feeling these losses the heaviest? Who was carrying Bowie's or Prince's lyrics with them the most? Whose grief was the most likable, shareable? The attention economy does not make room for the laborious undertaking of embracing and reckoning with ugly feelings, and so social media trades on grief as though each post, each tweet, were a step in the grieving process and not an elision of that very process.

In this spirit, Lady Gaga – preferring ink to digital characters – had the cover of Bowie's 1973 album *Aladdin Sane* tattooed onto her left ribs. She documented the process on Snapchat for good measure, and later dressed like Ziggy Stardust to a Grammys after-party to honour the late rock star. These acts served to foreground and reiterate how important Bowie was to Gaga, who wanted to demonstrate the intimacy she felt with the late singer. Even if that intimacy was one-sided. To some people (including one of Bowie's former bandmates, and the rock star's son), these gestures of tribute and their documentation on social media came across as Gaga capitalizing on Bowie's death, invoking his name and inking his face onto her body as a way of amalgamating his fame with her own waning status as offbeat icon.

And yet, it might also be worthwhile to consider the ways that grief can be simultaneously felt *and* performed. Not all grieving needs to be experienced alone, cloistered in the dark. Gaga's need to wear her grief on the surface of her skin does not automatically make that grief superficial. The boldness of her broadcast sorrow makes me think that perhaps she is not unlike Antigone, a symbol of both feeling and action. It might be tacky, it might be tender, it might be strategic – or Gaga's grief might just point to the contradiction of modern mourning: a compulsion to rapidly articulate that which is so hard to put into words. Bonus if that articulation doubles as shareable viral content.

The trouble with the iteration of mourning we can find online is that compared to the important work of eulogizing a life, it is but a quick fix to what is perceived as the problem or bad luck of death. What's more, the user who gets to the keyboard first and breaks the news is transformed by her timely tweet into Top Griever. Top Griever becomes a personal news source to others who can turn to her for the best archived photo of Bowie, of Prince, and retweet that to their own followers with the comfort of knowing that the grief content they are sharing has been vetted.

While there is comfort in being a part of the conversation, feeling a part of something bigger than yourself, there's also something socially compulsive about the rush to memorialize a dead celebrity online. A hint of surveillance; a whiff of the hegemonic. When there is a compulsion to commemorate and to profess one's sadness in the wake of a famous figure's death, online mourning becomes just another script we are meant to follow. To hashtag-RIP a celeb you saw in a movie twenty years ago because that's what the well-branded avatars you follow online are doing is not to grieve. It is to perform a version of grief that carries with it some virtual currency, some sense of social cachet. Grief is performed on social media as part of an unspoken competition to grieve the most beautifully, eloquently, and intimately across platforms. This intimacy is illusory.

To be clear, not all intimacy produced through social media is imagined; affinities are discovered and bonds forged daily and even lastingly through the internet. But an intimacy arising from public performances of grief is an intimacy run amok.

With this version of social media sorrow, there comes an expectation – nay, a duty – to memorialize the famous in order to feel connected to your networks, and the assumption that underlies this duty is that we are all mourning (and ought to mourn) the same thing. Coupled with this homogenization of grief and where it lands is the familiar impetus to grieve quickly, efficiently, swiftly. Online there is a need to be timely in your mournful gesturing – get that content out there and get it circulating, strike while the iron is hot. Once again the link between information and consumer capitalism is razor-sharp: the user, the magazine, the newspaper, the brand that can find the right hook, or persuade the most clicks, gains the most currency if their timing is right. Currency is both symbolic of social aptitude – an ability to massage the temples of the zeitgeist just so – and, in the case of Twitter and Facebook, the literal money made off our collective grief-sharing. Even tear-lined eyes are counted for advertising impressions.

The grief-news cycle has begun to churn at a quick clip. When Princess Diana died in 1997, the pre-internet public outpouring expanded into weeks. Twelve years later, when Michael Jackson died in 2009, sites like Google, Twitter, and Facebook experienced a major strain and there was danger of 'breaking' the internet. Before then, reports the *Telegraph*, 'the last time there was such strain put on the web was in the aftermath of 9/11.' In 2012, when Whitney Houston died, a number of news stations – CNN, MSNBC, and Fox News – halted their regularly scheduled programming upon hearing confirmed reports of her death and began their non-stop coverage. By winter 2016 and the deaths of Prince and Bowie, the news cycle grew tighter still. Before too long, news stations covering these celebrity deaths ran out of material. Writers of internet hot takes couldn't find enough new angles on the same story and so moved on to new, more relevant topics. Grief doesn't make for a good story arc because it begins right at the end. There are only so many times you can go back and tell the story of a loss from the beginning as a matter of entertainment.

Collectively eulogizing a celebrity has the patina of intimacy, but how brittle a bond! The solitary mourner has no interest in remaining relevant or entertaining, doesn't mind replaying that story over and over. In the gauziness of my own grief, the time never seemed right to talk about my mom's last words of advice for her kids (she told us, simply, 'Love one another'), the excruciating pain she felt in her final few days, or the way she mouthed my brother's name as she slipped in and out of consciousness. Those weren't stories anyone seemed particularly interested in hearing. 'What will you do next?' was the question I got asked the most. 'Miss her every day and learn to live with a gaping lack at the centre of my self and search for home in each new person I meet' would have been a more honest answer than the blank stare I usually gave. In this seemingly innocuous question that extended family and friends asked me was, I felt, an insistence that I look only forward and not back. I needed to plan for the future and adapt to it without my mom, and I needed to do that immediately. I was staring up at a wall of immense grief, and the people around me were asking that I explain what lay on the other side of it.

Each time the story of loss is told, it is experienced as an encounter with what has been lost – and for me there's comfort in that. It's sort of like dreaming of the person you miss terribly – the dream might not be particularly comforting, and waking up with the realization that the person is gone certainly isn't a balm, but there's a feeling that ambles around in the mind that you've been near your loved one in a way that the waking world doesn't permit. The writer Alex Ronan experienced an intensely personal loss at the same time that the whole internet, or so it seemed, was busy grieving a series of newly dead celebrities. Ronan's grief chafed against the claims of online users that they were experiencing the death of David Bowie – a stranger – as a tragedy. A few days after the memorial for her younger brother, Mark, in January 2016, Ronan was confronted with post after post about the death of Bowie every time she went online. Over the phone, she explained to me that 'when you lose someone that you love, you feel like the whole world should stop, and everyone on the planet should go into mourning. The death feels so huge that it doesn't make sense that people are still going to the grocery store or complaining about their friends […] so then to see the whole world mourning someone else feels like a punch in the gut.'

Before losing Mark, Ronan had already been thinking and writing about online grief and the rise of social media mourning. With experience culled from both research and now her own reaction, Ronan surmises that 'there's not enough space for grieving and mourning. Growing attached to a celebrity's death is a way for people to grab onto that process without making themselves really vulnerable.' Ronan reflects on the formulaic responses that get pushed out on Twitter, Facebook, and Instagram when someone famous dies, noting that 'a lot of the time it seems more and more like people are writing less about the person that died and more about themselves.' She sees it as people peering over into the lake of loss and dipping their toe in from the safety of firmer ground: 'It gives people a way to take a bit of space to be the griever, but also to not have to get too close to death.' She explains the difference between grieving a celebrity online versus grieving someone more intimate by saying, 'The distance of mourning a celebrity – everyone can share in that – and that way you don't have to get into the nitty-gritty discomfort of really dealing with someone whose sibling, or father, or mom has died. It's not you writing on Facebook about your dead grandmother over and over again.'

Online grieving is finite, Ronan reminds us. Personal grief is infinite. There is no door to close and leave your grief behind when that grief is yours and yours alone. When it's your brother, your mom, your kid, you can't simply tweet, or share, or link away the pain. You can't just close your browser and move on with your day. 'I hate the thought that there should be a timeline to grief, and I try to reject that,' Ronan tells me. 'I want to take as much time as I need, and as long as Mark's gone I will be mourning him – I feel so much pressure to be "better" or to pick up my life again, but I don't want to be "better"; it takes me further away from Mark.' She adds, 'You know, people talk about the stages of grief, and I can't relate to that because I think grief moves in waves rather than in a straight linear progression. I don't think you can put a timeline on something that moves in waves.' What's more, she doesn't 'want something that wraps up in a year. I want grieving to be a part of my everyday life.'

These public gesticulations of grief online – performative rites and rituals through which we understand death – have a real impact on the expectations surrounding private mourning. That is, the way that people have come to mourn publicly for celebrities has become an insidious blueprint for mourning more personal losses. To frame this idea in slightly different terms, grieving a figure like Bowie (very publicly, very emotion-ally, but most of all very *quickly*) becomes a model for how we ought to grieve those more intimate to us whom we lose. Share your loss online, post old photos and revisit cherished anecdotes, continue this for one or two days, and then move on. The stark limit to public eulogizing that we see on social media is indicative of a more deeply entrenched notion that we ought to quickly 'get over' loss and get back to work. This relationship to grief – a *get it out and get it over with* attitude – is easy enough to find in the self-help aisle of your local big box store. From *Getting to the Other Side of Grief*, to *How to Heal a Broken Heart in 30 Days*, to the triumphantly titled *Conquering Grief*, there is an expiry date on how long you can grieve, and these books will help you meet your deadline.

Toronto writer Claire Wilmot discovered this crass new way of mourning – which mimics the social media sorrow outpouring we see for celebrities – the day after her sister Lauren's death in March 2016. Writing in the *Atlantic*, Wilmot describes the loss of Lauren as the feeling of a hole being ripped in her universe. While trying to piece together a world newly void of her sister, Wilmot discovered that distant acquaintances of Lauren had already begun the social media mourning. Wilmot writes that

> across the city, a former classmate of Lauren's learned of her death... The classmate selected what is perhaps the only picture of the two of them together, and decided to post it on Lauren's timeline. Beneath it, she wrote 'RIP' and something about heaven gaining an angel.

What happened next, you might have guessed. The social media post became the way many of Lauren's close friends learned that she had died.

> We – her family – hadn't yet been able to call people. The first post sparked a cascade of status updates and

pictures, many from people who barely knew her. It was as though an online community felt the need to claim a stake in her death, through syrupy posts that profoundly misrepresented who she was and sanitized what had happened to her. Lauren was an intensely private person, not one to identify with her diagnosis – a rare form of neurological cancer. She would have had little patience for the mawkish tributes on social media that followed.

As this instance makes evident, online grieving can go horribly awry. It's not just that rushing to announce death online can be incredibly vulgar – though it is certainly that; these swift acts of eulogizing can also override the wishes for privacy of those who are actually in the midst of mourning, those who are doing the labour of piecing their worlds back together and taking stock of its new cracks. As Wilmot points out, the impulse to share and link to death also sanitizes the pain and illness that were its very cause. Clichés about heaven gaining an angel and sentiments about the deceased being 'too good for this world' paper over the actual experience – in this instance, Lauren's experience – of dying.

We live in a culture where the ill and the dying are largely kept out of sight and experiences of loss are elided. Barbara Ehrenreich has repeatedly pointed out that cancer patients are often spoken of in terms of survival rather than sickness. In a 2010 piece for the *Guardian*, for example, she explains:

As in the AIDS movement, upon which breast cancer activism is partly modelled, the words 'patient' and 'victim,' with their aura of self-pity and passivity, have been ruled un-PC. Instead, we get verbs: those who are in the midst of their treatments are described as 'battling' or 'fighting', sometimes intensified with 'bravely' or 'fiercely' – language suggestive of Katharine Hepburn with her face to the wind.

Using the language of the fight implies a matter of will, of control. Dying from a terminal disease is not a choice. Death cannot be overcome, and implying that if only one is capable of a great feat of strength they should live forever is the exact kind of lie that allows us, the living, to avoid reckoning with the painful truth.

When Bowie's death was announced in slightly longer form on his professional Facebook page, it was revealed that the star had been slowly dying in private for a year and a half: 'David Bowie died peacefully today surrounded by his family after a courageous 18 month battle with cancer. While many of you will share in this loss, we ask that you respect the family's privacy during their time of grief.' His illness was divulged in retrospect and it was revealed that his family had been anticipating their loss for months. Bowie's public, who professed their love for him and laid claim to an intimacy mediated by his music, were confronted with the reality of their icon's private life – something which, they had to admit, they knew nothing about. The revelation of Bowie's liver cancer caused critics and fans to reframe his final album, *Blackstar*, as the artist's swan song, his 'parting gift' (as his producer Tony Visconti called it) to his fans. It was as if Bowie were eulogizing himself from beyond the grave. The album was released on his sixty-ninth birthday, two days before his death.

Much like Duncan Jones's note that he would be offline for 'a while' to grieve, this Facebook post even more deliberately asked for privacy during the family's 'time of grief.' Just how long is a time of grief? How long is a while? It's difficult to do the arithmetic of mourning since 'forever' isn't a socially acceptable answer, and yet grief doesn't go away; the time of grief is continually unfolding for those who have lost, and 'a while' can stretch far into the future. Sometimes the only thing that feels certain about the future is that it will be marked by the grief one feels now. For those mourning the idea of Bowie, and not the man David Jones, there was no need to take time for grief, there was no need to be offline for a while. According to *Billboard*, 'within the first 12 hours of news that David Bowie had died on Sunday, 35 million people had 100 million interactions about the rock icon's passing on Facebook.'

In contemplation of the socially sanctioned impulse to announce, share, and compete in the news of a celebrity's death, and the general elision of loss more broadly, perhaps it's no wonder that mourning through social media strikes me as a fraught enterprise. Yet, there must be ways of grieving online as in life that, born of original feeling and critical thinking, gets us close to that ongoing struggle for authenticity. To want to express emotion genuinely in language is not a new desire – it was not manufactured by Mark Zuckerberg; Steve Jobs holds no purchase over it. Rather, finding the words, especially the last ones, is a necessary and loving task. To eulogize is to say out loud that a life is not forgotten when it crosses the threshold into death. It means something to those left to grieve it, and the attempt to encapsulate that life in an act of articulation is one of the truest labours of love there is.

There are ways in which online commemorations do function as the eulogy is meant to: to offer some words of comfort and memory on the occasion of a death. For instance, Sarah Nicole Prickett wrote a profound tribute to Bowie in her TinyLetter. Of the acts and articulations of commemoration for Bowie, Prickett remarks:

No sentiment is too grand for The Man Who Fell To Earth, 'that outsider who made different kids feel like dancing in that difference,' as [Hilton] Als says, 'and who had a genius for friendship, too,' and who, let me add, gave integrity and art to careerism, yet the idea that he was born to not die is one I can't stand. Not only does it run counter to what Bowie assumed about his own life, it also elides how difficult it could be for him to live. How improbable it became that he'd still be alive at 30, and what sizable triumphs, especially over his own will, it took for him to get to 69.

Further to Prickett's point, the popular notion of Bowie's thwarted immortality runs counter not only to his own perception of his time on earth but to all of our time on earth. This is not to be understood in the trite carpe diem sense of death; Bowie's death is not an impetus to open your eyes and really start living your life. Bowie's death should be about the fact that David Jones is now dead. Losing a figure like Bowie is tough, but, as Prickett makes clear, the living is hard, too. Let's not forget that. When virtual eulogies like this one narrow in on the specific life now lost, they hold open a space online to grieve a bit longer, and I have no doubt that this virtual act of memorialization brought comfort to those grieving Bowie, constellating their loss alongside Prickett's expression of a shared feeling.

Our relationships to the famous are only ever fantastical. Our connections to them are from the very start imagined on our part and girded by our repeated encounter with that figure in film, music, and other media. Over time our encounters with, for example, Prince accrue to form the semblance of a correspondence: an analogical link that likens their queerness to ours, that bridges the gap between their unfathomable talent and wealth and our small lives. We peer into the pool not looking for our own reflection, but to glimpse, as if from the depths, the icon who we like to dream is looking right back and just as deeply. Where things get thorny is not when grief is guided by narcissism (what is more intimate to us than our loss?), but rather when that introspection and sorrow is quickly displaced in favour of simple, easy-to-process, and quick-to-pass emotions. When we mourn online in order to take solace in how far our tweet has gone or how many likes our post has gotten, we sidestep the ugly work of feeling bad.

The Futility of Progress

You can't set a deadline for grief because loss has no temporal limit; the clock will never run out. Certainly, a relationship exists between time and grief, though it is not teleological; rather, there is an alchemy that occurs, altering how the bereaved experiences each. The change isn't a dramatic clap of combustion, but a slow, sometimes imperceptible, transformation. What time revealed to me is that grieving is lasting and it is forever, but it is not immutable. With days, and weeks, and months, and years, and then a decade, the razor-sharp edges of my grief began to dull. Over time, the acute sting of losing my mom deepened into a generalized ache. It's not that I feel my loss less keenly than before, but that my grief is no longer a weight bearing down on both my shoulders; it no longer quite pins me in place. My sorrow has enmeshed itself in cross-hatched strands into the everyday texture of my life.

I've never wanted to lose hold of my grief or to shake it off. Even at the nadir of my despair, when I felt like there was no firm ground left to stand on, I knew I didn't want to get over it. Amid this disorientation, my grief has sometimes felt like the only thing I truly knew about myself. Losing my mom, I became broken – a fact I held with complete certitude. Learning to live with loss has also been learning to live with brokenness.

Time didn't 'teach' me this about grief: time isn't didactic and grief isn't a case study. In rethinking our relationship to loss, it becomes impossible to avoid encountering a paradox: we tend to think of temporality in linear terms and increments, but grief doesn't proceed like that. Neither does time, despite what we've learned to believe about chronology. We think of time as easily divisible and categorizable, and that same structure has been imposed on grief, which is described in 'stages' and subject to socially understood timelines – whether you're tweeting about Prince or instagramming a photo of your dead dad, there comes a point where one's public mourning is meant to cease. But linearity is a concept we have grafted onto time, probably so that it feels less immense to us. I can imagine the first craftsmen chiselling sundials out of rock with a sense that they were making the vast, largely mysterious universe slightly less so by divvying it up. Cutting the light of day into comprehensible pie-sized slices may have steeled them against their total insignificance and lack of existential control. For perhaps the same reasons, we continue to insist on and reiterate the notion that time is linear, sequential, and easily segmented. And we likewise insist that grief follow a linear progression. The compulsion to slot grief into divisible stages along a narrow path is to ward off an overwhelming feeling of total engulfment. The jarring irony is that by attempting to make temporality more manageable, we have cultivated a punishing relationship to time and a more restrictive relationship to grief.

French philosopher Henri Bergson's theory of time, first published in 1922 as *Duration and Simultaneity*, debunks the scientific idea that temporality can be measured. Bergson figures that science and mathematics are insufficient for measuring time because the instant you try to measure a moment, that moment has already passed. He highlights what traditional accounts of temporality don't permit, which is its ineffability – the impossibility of pinning it down long enough to measure. Time is fluid, and like Heraclitus's river, once you've waded a foot into it, it has already moved, changed. 'No two moments are identical in a conscious being,' as Bergson would have it. Instead of thinking of time in linear terms, he offers us his theory of time as duration (*la durée*), which accounts for an intuitive relation to time and how it passes. Though we are always free (and often inclined) to believe we can split and cordon off time, the movement of time is itself indivisible. By this Bergsonian reasoning, if time is ineffable, then it is a fool's errand to insist on its measurability. Likewise, grief has *duration*, so to think of it in terms of progress is futile. Once you've experienced grief, it becomes eponymous – it is everywhere you look, it is in everything you do – and it verges on the fringe of absurd to insist on grief's completion when that grief is in everything.

Bergson explains that time is best accounted for in images, which is to say we can get closer to conceiving of time when we use our imagination and our intuition. The writer David Foster Wallace gives us an image that demonstrates Bergson's *durée* in his short story 'Good Old Neon' from his 2004 collection, *Oblivion*. Near the end of the story the narrator, who has, in a sense, been delivering an extended meta-eulogy while sitting in the passenger seat of another's car, puts it this way:

> One clue that there's something not quite real about sequential time the way you experience it is the various paradoxes of time supposedly passing and of a so-called 'present' that's always unrolling into the future and creating more and more past behind it. As if the present were this car – nice car by the way – and the past is the road we've just gone over, and the future is the headlit road up ahead we haven't yet gotten to, and time is the car's forward movement, and the precise present is the car's front bumper as it cuts through the fog of the future, so that it's *now* and then a tiny bit later a whole different *now*, etc.

Wallace doesn't completely disregard the idea of temporal chronology (the car is moving forward, after all), but he puts his finger on the 'not quite real' aspect of the present moment. The past and the future are a bit easier to grasp, but the present is ineffable. Wallace's front bumper cutting through 'the fog of the future' is akin to a Bergsonian foot in the flowing river: *now* cannot be measured, it can only be experienced in its anticipation and in its fleetingness. Like these conceptions of time, there is something 'not quite real' about how we conceive of grief and our processing of it – we require images and intuition to wrap our heads around what it means to be in a state of perpetual mourning. While time is impossible to measure because of its fleeting nature, grief can be confounding in its lastingness.

When you are pressured to get over grief in a timely fashion, time itself begins to feel restrictive, like the tightening straps of a straitjacket that draw your arms incrementally closer, as though you might suffocate yourself in a lonely embrace. The canvas begins to chafe and your joints begin to pulse with each moment that grief's lastingness goes unacknowledged.

With time's grip around you, expectations dictate when grieving should be done, or the stages your mourning should proceed through on its way toward *completion*. The rites and incantations and sad carnations of the funeral tradition are sanctioned steps in the conventional grieving process that buttress the notion that grief is measurable. These rituals are not inherently flawed but, like the eulogy, they are not often given any room to breathe, expand, or fill up too much space. Funerals are characterized by the constraint of time – they are last-minute, often rushed events, and can feel like one more notch being tightened against the expansiveness of grief.

While the funeral oration goes back as far as Ancient Greece, it wasn't until the fifteenth century that the word *eulogy* came into regular usage. In terms of its Greek root, it means exactly what you might think: the word comes from *eulogia*, which means to praise. The conventional eulogy praises the dead in part because of the precise historical moment at which the eulogy emerged; not all dead bodies were grieved publicly in Ancient Greece, so the ones that *were* chosen to be memorialized were deemed worthy of public mourning and thereby praiseworthy. If you were grieved publicly, you must have been a man of great repute and power, and the eulogy functioned to celebrate those successes.

An early example of eulogy as not only praise, but as an act of poetic justice or reparation, comes from William Basse in 1641. Writing in honour of William Shakespeare twenty-five years after the playwright's death, Basse's address occurs following a delay that we don't typically associate with the eulogy. Part of what makes the contemporary eulogy such a challenging and often daunting task is the swiftness with which it needs to be delivered. For the eulogizer, there's hardly any time to pause, catch her breath, and reflect on what she's lost before the moment has come to stand up and deliver this public praise. Instead of a eulogy that solely lauds Shakespeare for his great works, Basse penned a sonnet chastising the reading public for not recognizing the bard's genius sooner. Consider the opening lines of 'On Mr. Wm. Shakespeare, he died in April 1616':

> Renowned Spenser, lie a thought more nigh
> To learned Chaucer, and rare Beaumont lie
> A little nearer Spenser to make room
> For Shakespeare in your threefold, fourfold tomb.
> To lodge all four in one bed make a shift
> Until Doomsday, for hardly will a fifth
> Betwixt this day and that by fate be slain
> For whom your curtains may be drawn again.

Here, Basse is suggesting that a little graveyard shuffling of the great poets buried in Westminster Abbey should occur, making room for Shakespeare's corpse. Spenser's body should move a little to the left, an expired Chaucer ought to cozy up to him, and Beaumont needs to scooch over so that Shakespeare can take his rightful place in the famous dead poets' society. Recognizing the period's dual functions of eulogy – to praise publicly and to chronicle great men – Basse writes one for Shakespeare as a way of penning him into a more prestigious history than his humble beginnings had allowed for. In the sonnet's second half, Basse acquiesces that even though the dead refuse to move, Shakespeare will still be Shakespeare regardless of where he lies:

> If your precedency in death doth bar
> A fourth place in your sacred sepulcher,
> Under this carved marble of thine own
> Sleep rare tragedian Shakespeare, sleep alone,
> Thy unmolested peace, unshared cave,
> Possess as lord not tenant of thy grave,
> > That unto us and others it may be
> > Honor hereafter to be laid by thee.

Instead of appealing to the more famous poets who take up Westminster Abbey's prime real estate, Basse here changes his tune, deciding that Shakespeare may well be better off on his own. He ends his sonnet by earmarking a future moment in history when people and poets alike will clamour to be buried not in the open green of the Abbey, but close to Shakespeare.

This tradition of praising the dead has persisted even in the more democratized form of the eulogy, which is perhaps why it feels as though there is no room for any fraught or troubled or confused feelings when we first give public language to our private losses. Since the *eulogia* is a speech of praise, it is from the very start only half the story of the dead – none of our lives, even those of the most monastic among us, are without ugliness. And because praise is only part of the story of our lives, the eulogy splinters from an authentic account of the dead before it is even written. The reason the contemporary eulogy rings false or falters in its dependence on cliché is because it is a mode of address meant as a vehicle of *only* praise. The eulogy's infidelity to the nuance, ambiguity, and intricacies of a life – things frankly absent from even the most compelling list of the deceased's accolades – gives way to a second, more problematic pitfall. Since the eulogy is meant to praise the so-called great men of society, it finds itself rooted in a hierarchy of grievability – that is, the eulogy has historically been tied to a hegemonic categorization of whose life is seen as grievable and whose, well, is not.

It is still common to grieve certain bodies publicly and not others. With the Black Lives Matter movement rippling across the U.S., there is a vocal collective of activists and regular folk protesting the many systemic ways in which Black life is not seen as worthy of preserving in the first instance and mourning in the second. By insisting that Black life does in fact matter, the movement is also insisting that the brutal extinguishing of that life by police and the George Zimmermans of the world is a matter of public and judicial significance. The outpouring of anger and very public grief at Black Lives Matter demonstrations is an avowal of the grievability of Black life and, therefore, the praiseworthiness of that life, too.

When Beyoncé Knowles chose to feature Sybrina Fulton, Lesley McSpadden, and Gwen Carr in her visual album *Lemonade* in 2016, she was eulogizing murdered Black life in America. These women are the mothers of Trayvon Martin, Michael Brown, and Eric Garner – all unarmed Black men killed for no other discernible reason than the fact that they were Black. The presence of these women – each holding a framed photo of her dead son as the glow of a fire casts their faces in orange and amber shadows – in Beyoncé's most political album to date is an integral statement about the worthiness of those lives. This sequence of the visual album is accompanied by the languid ballad 'Forward' with James Blake, a succinct twelve-line song that insists on both poise and action. The delicate, trembling tempo of this extended scene is followed by the final act of the album and the rousing anthem 'Freedom,' featuring Kendrick Lamar. In it, Beyoncé promises that her tears will turn to fire – her sadness combusting into something volatile, unapologetic, and red-hot. By choosing to move into the redemptive verses of 'Freedom,' Beyoncé accentuates the anger that will coincide with any movement forward, political, personal, or, as second-wave feminism taught us, both. Beyoncé's adamantly public eulogy for the unsung lives of Martin, Brown, and Garner is a niche of grief that she has tenaciously carved out, urging an audience of millions to pause and to reflect over their loss, and to praise these men.

The lasting power of loss, and the time of grief, fascinated Sigmund Freud; the father of psychoanalysis wrote about and returned to this grim material throughout his prolific career, constantly revising his theory of mourning. In his theory's earliest iteration, Freud writes that grief work needs to come to an end before too much time has passed. Freud believed that grief is disorienting and can turn the world as you've known it upon its head, but it can't last forever. Or maybe a more accurate summary of Freud's thinking is to say that he knew that grief could and would last forever if you let it, so the trick was not to let it. His essential 1917 essay 'Mourning and Melancholia' warns against prolonged mourning, lest the griever slip into the paralyzing depths of melancholia.

The lines Freud draws are rigid, in part because he was trying to make a science out of the slippery landscapes of our interior lives. He set out to chart some coordinates of this vast psychic space with the recognizable and measurable tools of science. As it turns out, one of science's favourite tools is pathologization – the categorizing of anything other than 'normal' as some form of sickness, ailment, or aberration.

That's what extended grief came to be associated with: an emotional illness that was counterproductive and pesky for modern civilization. By 1923, Freud had changed his mind about the timeliness of grief work; in *The Ego and the Id*, he describes how the losses we experience accrue over time like a sediment on our character – gently but surely changing the makeup of who we are. Freud's thought evolved and deepened over the years, but his initial thoughts on mourning are emblematic of a narrative that has persisted from his era to our own: that there isn't enough time for grief. Even in the wake of loss, things must proceed like business as usual. Those who refuse to proceed as such or, less boisterously, simply can't get back to work, are deemed stubborn melancholics who dwell in their sadness.

I've spent the past few years investigating and theorizing the importance of the melancholic's steadfastness to loss. As a PhD student, I combed through contemporary fiction, film, and critical theory looking for characters, artists, and thinkers who rejected the happiness scripts of modern life. I found the work of Sara Ahmed, Barbara Ehrenreich, David Eng, José Muñoz, Jack Halberstam – all of whom skewer the forced optimism that undergirds American politics, consumerism, and talk of 'healthy lifestyles.' These thinkers underscore the systemic ways that this moral attitude, characterized by progress, efficiency, and the forward quest for happiness, denies and pathologizes feelings of sadness and disenfranchisement. Over the course of my study, I analyzed and envied the idea of rebelling against the status quo of possessing an emotional life that requires a relinquishing of loss in the service of productivity and efficiency. What would it mean to allow myself to be sad for as long as I needed? What would it mean to not be propelled by the romance of progress? My mom died in November of 2004 and I returned to school within two weeks and was caught up on missed work by Christmas.

I went on to write a research project for my Master's degree, and then a PhD dissertation, on modern grief. The irony is not lost on me that by pursuing two graduate degrees I had turned my own work of mourning into something *useful*.

From a safe theoretical distance, I analyzed and critiqued the way that, as subjects living in late-stage capitalism, we are confronted with an unspoken ethical duty to be a contributing and productive member of society in pursuit of the good life. I studied Freud on mourning, I read Lacan on lack, I considered Derrida's reflections on mortality, and I looked to art for more capacious understandings of grief. I did all of this with as little introspection as I could get away with and wrote a rigorous and well-received dissertation.

Finishing that project made me reckon with the reality that I needed to now *practice* my theory of melancholy. I was wrapping up my academic investigation into mourning and I needed to find a way of being in the world – the actual world I lived in – that included and made room for the accumulated sediment of my grief because, it was startlingly clear to me now, it wasn't going anywhere.

Writing about my grief has changed my relationship to it. Despite my many attempts to avoid the painful work of processing my loss more intimately, writing about my grief cracked it wide open again. Finishing my dissertation felt like 'finishing' my work of mourning, because regardless of how much I have theoretically rejected a linear narrative of grief, I have still felt compelled to obey its rules. I didn't want to be done with grief, but at the same time I *did* want to be done with the first twelve years of mourning because I'm sure they were the hardest, the rawest, and the loneliest I will know.

When the poet William Wordsworth eulogized a friend in an early-nineteenth-century verse, he aptly called his poem 'After-Thought,' nodding to the fact that grief takes some time to settle, like the silt that gets kicked up and clouds a still pond. Some measure of clarity – a grasp on what in reality is now gone – doesn't happen in a timely fashion. Wordsworth acknowledges that grief abides, and like the River Duddon that he likens his sorrow to, it will 'forever glide' because 'The Form remains' and 'the Function never dies.' A century after Wordsworth's heartfelt eulogy in verse, Freud expressed a similar understanding of the longevity of grief in a short essay called 'On Transience.'

Written in 1915, when World War I was wreaking havoc on the civilization Freud and his contemporaries had taken for granted, the essay begins with an anecdote about walking through a garden with a poet – rumoured to be Rainer Maria Rilke – who was completely distraught by the bald realization that nothing lasts, and that the people we love are perishable. Freud recounts that this pessimistic poet was

> disturbed by the thought that all this beauty was fated to extinction, that it would vanish when winter came, like all human beauty and all the beauty and splendour that men have created or may create. All that he would otherwise have loved and admired seemed to him to be shorn of its worth by the transience that was its doom.

While he abstains from making false promises that the doom the poet fears won't descend – both men were in the midst of processing the destruction of war: doom had already arrived – Freud's response is uniquely optimistic. Avowing the loss that surrounds him, he writes that the transience of what is beautiful or what we love in no way diminishes its worth – 'On the contrary, an increase!' Arguing a point I find irrefutable, Freud continues: 'Limitation in the possibility of an enjoyment raises the value of the enjoyment. It was incomprehensible, I declared, that the thought of the transience of beauty should interfere with our joy of it.' Just because things don't last doesn't mean we love them any less, or could even if we tried. Freud's point is that not only does transience *not* get in the way of our loving, the fact that we are mortal is what makes loving possible to begin with. If we had lifetimes or centuries to care for people, would we set out to do it right away? Humans are born procrastinators; our transience is a deadline that motivates us to bother with the messy, chaotic, painful, and blissful labour of loving other people.

Even so, 'On Transience' ends on a utilitarian note. Freud likens the personal losses we face over a lifetime to those 'caused by this war' and hopes that 'once the mourning is over, it will be found that our high opinion of the riches of civilization has lost nothing from our discovery of their fragility.' Freud is still pushing this idea that mourning follows a linear path, with a beginning and an end. He also collapses the intimate losses we might experience when a loved one dies with the collective horror of war – to put it another way, Freud tells his reader that a shared idea of loss and the personal feelings of loss are the same thing. Like many of Freud's essays and case studies, 'On Transience' concludes with its author trying to tie up all the ideas presented with a declarative bow. Freud had a tendency in his writing to explore the nuance of a psychological complexity or neurosis only to then rebuke that expansive line of inquiry with a decisiveness I have difficulty imagining he sincerely felt. (I've always chalked these moments up to a pandering Freud must have thought necessary for the audience of scientists he was often writing for. I imagine the need to prove a hypothesis is a difficult impulse to shake, even when you know that matters are much more tangled than that.)

We can't pin everything on Freud; even before his theories of kink, narcissism, and the transience of beauty worked their way into European thought, certain political efficiencies were already associated with grief, and with the eulogy in particular. In the U.S., when Abe Lincoln died in 1865, public grieving began to emerge as the celebrity sport that only now, with the rise of social media, has reached its fever pitch. Not that the public mourning of President Lincoln wasn't aided and influenced by the period's technology: the development of the railroad and the arrival of telephone lines literally connected the news of Lincoln's death to the American population. People and news were travelling faster than ever, and that meant a different sort of national identity was beginning to take root, a constantly evolving sense of Americanness that was emerging in the waning days of the Civil War as the country's strict North and South divide reluctantly buckled and the work of Reconstruction began.

The new flow of information was a part of this national identity as, for the first time in the history of the United States, citizens across the vast country began to receive news of current events at roughly the same time. Lincoln's assassination was broadcast from coast to coast and from top to bottom, and soon headlines of his weeks-long funeral procession would become a regular news item everywhere. When Lincoln was shot, the Washington newspaper the *National News* published the succinct headline 'Lincoln Shot: Condition Considered Hopeless, Will Not Live Through Night Doctors Declare' with his portrait wreathed in an American flag. The wave of cross-country mourning, chronicled in newspapers nationwide, followed from there.

The public outpouring of grief that met Lincoln's death almost certainly also had to do with his efforts to legislate against slavery. His place in the process of reconciling with the particular history of America's greatest, most shameful tragedy made his death mean many different things – both as a symbolic matter and a practical one – and gave him a popular celebrity previously unknown by any other American president.

In death, Lincoln became a national spectacle of grief and unification as his corpse was transported across seven states by a train known as the 'Lincoln Special,' travelling 1,654 miles with its scheduled stops announced in local papers. When proclamations were published in the towns and villages along the route of the Lincoln Special, mayors like George B. Senter of Cleveland requested 'that all places of business be immediately closed for the day; that appropriate symbols of mourning be displayed from all buildings, and that the citizens meet in the public square.' This pageantry was not only witnessed in the 180 cities that welcomed the presidential corpse along its circuitous route to Illinois but also, thanks to new technologies like the stereoscope (an early 3-D camera, basically), caught in vivid detail and published in newspapers across the nation. These pictures show the streets of Albany, of Columbus, of Buffalo bustling with hundreds of mourners gathered outside and others stretching their arms out of windows in a collective public display of grief. A vaulted tent sits atop the elevated casket of the sixteenth president, drawn by horse through the swarms of mourners. American flags hug the columns in town squares and women hold parasols against the afternoon heat. In New York City a military procession takes over five city blocks along Broadway while the curbs of sidewalks disappear under the crowds.

These photos suggest that technology and grief have long been comfortable bedfellows, and that there is a history of using new means of communication to share in the pageantry of grieving. A glaring contemporary visual corollary to these scenes is the packed streets of London that stood in anticipation of Princess Diana's cortege. Or perhaps the spectacle of Lincoln's multi-state funeral march can find an even more contemporary twin in the mass outpouring of civil and circumspect RIP hashtags that live on, for now at least, in the ephemeral archive of Twitter following the death of beloved celebrities like Bowie or Leonard Cohen.

Dr. Phineas D. Gurley, Lincoln's Presbyterian pastor, summed up the slain president's popularity in the funeral sermon he first delivered in the White House, and later published in the *New York Times* on April 20, 1865. Gurley said, 'Probably no man since the days of Washington was ever so deeply and firmly embedded and enshrined in the very hearts of the people as Abraham Lincoln.'

Another eulogy for the president was delivered by Henry Champion Deming before the General Assembly of Connecticut and published that year as a monograph by A. N. Clark & Co., State Printers. Thinking along more instrumental lines than the pastor, Deming used this public platform as a way of reaffirming Lincoln's politics. Like Basse, who eulogized Shakespeare, Deming recognized the useful historical work his eulogy could do. Connecticut governor William Buckingham, in introducing Deming, taps into emotion, suggesting that there cannot be 'a correct history of this nation, as it has passed through this great struggle for existence, without the life of Abraham Lincoln, and without connecting his name with that immortal proclamation which gave freedom and manhood to four millions of bondmen.' But soon after Buckingham strikes this emotional chord, Deming shifts tone to say, 'It is difficult to descend from the fervor of these first impassioned outbursts of a world wide grief, to cool analysis and historic delineation. And yet that is the task before me.'

Since eulogies must only praise the dead, the eulogizer is arm-wrestled into being reductive about the life lived. This reductiveness finds its match in the tinkering with categorization that happens when a celebrity dies, be it Prince, President Lincoln, or Muhammad Ali. Despite the latter's vexed history of American allegiance – the famed boxer ruffled more than feathers when he converted to Islam and then dodged conscription to the Vietnam War – what was emphasized on the occasion of Ali's death was his status as national hero and world-renowned champion fighter. Despite the manifold ways Ali disrupted placid notions of what it meant to be an American, the tidy work of eulogizing firmly recast him as a national treasure. This public positioning of Ali in his death shows clearly how cutting out, with near-surgical clarity, a fixed identity for the person who now lies in rest requires doing-away with that person's real complexities, their brushes with ambiguity, all the contradictions that make up a self, a life.

In a related vein, Deming's eulogy for Lincoln went on to say that if he were to speak emotionally about the late president or his death, he would be violating 'the proprieties of this occasion,' regardless of how 'well deserved' those 'mere rhapsodies' may be. Instead of an indulgent eulogy, with messy, emotional expressions of allegiance and validation, Deming feels his role is to 'present an estimate of character to a Legislative body, and I can not forget that it habitually dwells in the mild atmosphere congenial to deliberation, that it solicits unvarnished statement instead of rhetorical flourish, and records its own judgment in the composed style of fact and argument.' By Deming's standards, the eulogy must be 'unvarnished,' and we encounter yet again a linguistic attempt to strip feeling away from public grief – a move that appears especially tone-deaf considering the pomp surrounding the president's two-week-long funeral procession.

The surge of public grief for Lincoln was contained by its extended procession schedule, and it doesn't offer a sustainable or usable model for how to grieve a more personal loss. It doesn't help to look at how a president was mourned to discern how you might begin to grieve someone you love. At worst, looking to public displays of grief will only emphasize the need to keep your mourning work to a minimum (fourteen days max) and to simplify your beloved for the sake of your audience. This pageantry, pomp, and praise for a national hero, which remains largely devoid of emotion and prone to historical categorization, is not helpful in understanding the private country of loss.

Here we are in the pews of a bright, white-walled church in the opening minutes of director Richard Curtis's beloved 2003 Christmas comedy *Love Actually*. An always-stoic Liam Neeson – playing the widower Daniel – begins to eulogize his late wife. With his signature lilting Irish tongue, Neeson mimics the heavy shoulders of a mourner, beaming a strained smile toward the funeral audience, hoping to find a comrade in the black-clad crowd as he performs the lonely work of eulogizing (luckily, Emma Thompson is there to smile back). He tells us that he and his wife, Joanna, had plenty of time to plan this service, signalling a prolonged illness that allowed for the couple to perform the grim work of event-planning while she slowly died. In advance of her death, Joanna determined that her eulogy would serve as a way of saying goodbye to her family and friends, and she chose to do this not through the commemorative words of her husband who would survive her, but rather, as Daniel puts it, 'ever so coolly, through the immortal genius of the Bay City Rollers.' Cue the upbeat harmonies of 'Bye Bye Baby,' playing over speakers and bouncing off the hallowed church walls, cue the pallbearers, cue the mix of knowing smiles and uncomfortable laughs from the funeral audience. A slide show plays behind the pulpit with photos of Joanna (played by an uncredited Rebecca Frayn) projected onto a white screen, a series of still images underscoring the spectral presence of the dead and making it seem almost as though she is presiding over her funeral from the beyond.

What's striking about this eulogy is not so much its musical component – though it *is* a discordant choice considering the song's subject is infidelity, containing – given the context – the regretful lines 'I could love you but why begin it/'Cause there ain't any future in it.' What's striking is the fact of the dead woman's anticipation of her eulogy and her orchestration of it. Everyone has time to prepare for his or her death in a general way, but not everyone has time to prepare for an imminent death – and what a bleak luxury that must be, to orchestrate one's own service. The plans that one hopes to have posthumously implemented (be it a musical eulogy or the redistribution of one's wealth) are made with a decisiveness that the decider has no way of enforcing. To try to plan your own eulogy is to try to arc time in your favour, to have things go your way just a little longer, even *after* your time has run out. The dead will not be there to see if her wishes get carried out or not, and yet she nonetheless makes requests for a future she will never see.

What's even more remarkable about Joanna's funeral plans is her preference to be eulogized through a popular song instead of from the lips of her beloved. Why leave the last words to be publicly spoken of you to a middling band from the 1970s? As much-loved as the song may be (or may have been, back in the day), how could it possibly hold more sentiment than words from your life partner, spoken in the wake of his losing you? Playing a pop song strikes me as a cagey move, buffering the fraught emotions of the mourners with commercial, mass-produced feeling. To prefer the sounds of 'Bye Bye Baby' over the words spoken by a lover is to attempt to mediate your death through clichéd lyrics rather than intimate experience. This mediation is a way of keeping the emotional intensity of loss at bay – to hold the pain of grief at arm's length and collapse it into a recognizable, upbeat narrative. In *Love Actually*, everyone in the audience looks dour because they have assembled to be sad. Yet, even at a funeral, where sadness is supposed to be socially permitted (the *one* release valve we have left!), even here a song is played to prompt the grievers to not be *too* sad.

Why displace the eulogy with a classic hit? Playing a pop song instead of listening to a personalized address could serve a few functions. It certainly adds some levity for the mourners – break the tension, lighten the mood. But why must Joanna's death be bubbly? Call it personal preference, but I want people to weep over my dead body when my time comes, not dance. Joanna wants to be commemorated lightheartedly, and perhaps to avoid having her illness define the terms of the proceedings.

My mom requested a similar elision, though thankfully without the cloyingly chipper soundtrack. She was adamant that her obituary not mention the cancer that killed her gradually over the course of two years and two days. Her illness had taken up so much space at the end of her life, not to mention swindling her out of a good three decades, give or take, and she didn't want the disease to overshadow or tinge the narrative of her life. I understood her point of view at the time, but I wish that she hadn't felt that worry. I wish she could have known that despite its very real physical consequences, cancer didn't diminish her. Cancer certainly didn't *undo* the story of her life, it just cut the story too short.

Neeson introducing his fictional wife's snappy musical eulogy also serves a formal function for the spectators of *Love Actually*. Closing a funeral scene with a pop hit keeps the pacing of the film relatively upbeat – 'Bye Bye Baby' concludes the moment of mourning with a wink and a nod that is in keeping with the film's flirty pace. Swiftly wrapping up the sombre funeral scene to the tune of the Bay City Rollers prevents this feel-good holiday movie from getting mired in the absolute ickiness of death. Plus, it saves the writers from needing to come up with meaningful words for a dispensable character. Eulogies are hard to write, even for people who don't exist.

Still, a funeral is not a situation that needs comedic diffusing – its tension is warranted, its lack of vim understandable. If the eulogy isn't the time and place to think about and articulate the importance of a life – however sad that task may be – then when? *Never* doesn't seem like a good enough answer. In another of Curtis's screenplays, though in this instance directed by Mike Newell, we see a character bristling at the difficulty of finding his own words to eulogize the dead. In *Four Weddings and a Funeral*, we watch as John Hannah, playing Matthew, eulogizes his partner, Gareth. It's not until the funeral scene that their relationship as lovers becomes clear to the audience. Matthew begins eulogizing by speaking of Gareth's joyfulness – he is the film's bon vivant, in blindingly colourful vests and a devilish grin – and considering how the mourners will collectively remember him. But when it is time for Matthew to speak of his private loss, it is there that he runs 'out of words.' Instead, he pleads: 'Perhaps you'll forgive me if I turn from my own feelings to the words of another splendid bugger: W. H. Auden. This is actually what I want to say.' Finding it easier to speak of Gareth in terms of a collective loss, Matthew is unable to muster the strength to speak to the intimacy of his own bereavement. Auden's poem 'Funeral Blues' is heartbreaking, there is no doubt, and it avoids the triteness of some other thematically related poems because it doesn't shirk grief's immensity:

> Stop all the clocks, cut off the telephone,
> Prevent the dog from barking with a juicy bone,
> Silence the pianos and with muffled drum
> Bring out the coffin, let the mourners come.
>
> Let aeroplanes circle moaning overhead
> Scribbling on the sky the message 'He is Dead.'
> Put crepe bows round the white necks of the public doves,
> Let the traffic policemen wear black cotton gloves.

He was my North, my South, my East and West,
My working week and my Sunday rest,
My noon, my midnight, my talk, my song;
I thought that love would last forever: I was wrong.

The stars are not wanted now; put out every one,
Pack up the moon and dismantle the sun,
Pour away the ocean and sweep up the wood;
For nothing now can ever come to any good.

Auden crafts the poem so that it spirals outward from the minutiae of domestic life to the wider world beyond – both of which are irrevocably changed, and worse off, now that 'He is Dead.' There is something so charming in the poet's petulance. His series of impossible commands are barely veiled confessions of his utter helplessness in the face of loss, and in each line and each hyperbole you can feel the vibration of his frustrated grief like twanging chords. Time itself is now useless to Auden. The tides are unnecessary, as is the moon that guides them. The laws of nature are moot to the griever, who feels life is unnatural without his lover. 'Funeral Blues' foregrounds the speaker's wish for the whole universe to weep for this one death and the heft of grief he feels. The dead was once the still point of the turning world for Auden, so the world no longer needs to turn. The cosmos serves no purpose anymore, and the poet feels as though all of life's crackle has fizzled with the extinguishing of this one life. Auden's exaggerations function as a salve. The poem's expansive images are there to try to match the simultaneous immensity and emptiness of feeling that comes with grief.

Yet, the choice of Matthew's prefacing words before reciting the poem is telling. Matthew asks to be forgiven for turning from his 'own feelings to the words of another.' This pivot from private feeling to a publicly shared text brings into relief the character's preference to displace his complicated and as yet unprocessed feelings of grief to the comforting coherence of Auden's four stanzas. Even though Matthew is at the church's pulpit to eulogize the person with whom he has built a life, he chooses to let the words of another do the talking.

Like 'Bye Bye Baby' in *Love Actually*, the incantation of 'Funeral Blues' also serves a pedestrian function. Auden's poem holds some poetic purchase and it functions just as well, if not better than, an original eulogy written specifically for the scene that might risk sounding too sappy or too simple. As *Love Actually* and *Four Weddings and a Funeral* make clear, the way to make the eulogy more enthralling is to draw on songs and lines that already have some credibility and popularity behind them (and for the love of pacing, keep these sad scenes short! There's a reason it's not *Four Funerals and a Wedding*).

When writer Norman Mailer published his own eulogy in a 1979 issue of *Boston*, twenty-eight years before he actually died, he was unabashedly trying to make death and the circumstances surrounding it entertaining. Mailer took it upon himself to do the work of eulogizing in advance of his death and seemed to delight in the task. 'Norman Mailer passed away yesterday after celebrating his fifteenth divorce and sixteenth wedding,' he writes, in the third person. Mailer continues commemorating himself in a mode that is part eulogy, part obituary, but mostly tongue-in-cheek self-mockery: 'At the author's bedside were eleven of his fifteen ex-wives, twenty-two of his twenty-four children, and five of his seven grandchildren, of whom four are older than six of their uncles and aunts.' As you can see, Mailer chose to make the subject of his own eulogy not his literary achievements but the splintered branches of his immediate family tree, which in turn highlights for the reader the author's strapping virility. Mailer might be 'dead' but his progeny live on, and so he casts male concupiscence as an eternal truth that stretches infinitely forward. The author's truest legacy is not his Pulitzer but the spawn that will continue to breathe in the oxygen he has at last, finally breathed out. Though hyperbolic, Mailer's piece crystallizes the arithmetic that underpins the planning that one does for death.

'At present, interest revolves around the estate,' continues Mailer.

> Noting that Executors have warned that Mailer, although earning an average income of one and a half million dollars a year, has had to meet an annual overhead of two million, three hundred thousand, of which two million, two hundred and fifty thousand went in child support, alimony, and back IRS payments. It is estimated that his liabilities outweigh his assets by eight million, six hundred thousand.

This distribution of his assets across ex-wives is what Mailer's self-imagined eulogy boils down to. The numbers: the number of his weddings and divorces, the number of his progeny, the number of his capital gains and debts, his back payments to the IRS. Basic math.

What Mailer's self-eulogizing and *Love Actually*'s Bay City Rollers eulogy share is an appreciation of the notion that the dead can shape the acts of commemoration that will follow on the heels of their death. These examples crystallize a wish to plan one's own funeral from the other side, when, by definition, commemoration is done by anyone *other* than us. Commemoration is literally 'a calling to remembrance, or preserving in memory, by some solemn observance, public celebration.' It's right there in the *OED*. What commemoration is not is a posthumous act of curation, no matter how much we desire to continue to shape our little corners of the world. To wit, we want immortality where there is none.

We want to exceed the limits of mortality because what a nuisance those limits are to us, as future-oriented animals. We thirst for a lastingness we can't have; we want influence where it has already perished; we want the future with us in it, someway, somehow. To plan your own funeral is narcissistic, but at that point, no one is going to call you on it.

Narcissism gets a bad name when, really, one's own death should be an important focal point of interest in our lives. When someone finds herself knowingly close to death, shouldn't she be allowed some narcissistic depths in which to wallow? Similarly, the person close to the dying or to the recently dead should be given a wide berth in which to dwell, sulk, mourn, stagnate, and crumple. Death is the time for self-indulgence. In a death-denying culture, it is little wonder that being introspective, even when reckoning with death, is deemed selfish and narcissistic. With this in mind, we might consider the fact that socially sanctioned permission to wallow may never come, and insisting on grief and its longevity is an uncomfortable, vital, and caring task.

There is a moment at the end of David Foster Wallace's 'Good Old Neon' that speaks to this primal desire to shape and manage how others see us even after we've died. This final narcissistic wish isn't a heinous character trait; it is, as the story reveals to us, simply a desire to be loved – and who can be faulted for that? 'Good Old Neon' is the story of Neal, a man so consumed by the idea that he is a fraud – and consequently incapable of having an authentic relationship with anyone – that he commits suicide. The story is told from the perspective of this already-dead protagonist, who recounts the story of his life to the reader, which is to say the events that led up to his painful end. Near the close of the narrative, Neal, who is by this point low-key-basking in the glow of death and feeling relatively sanguine about his fraudulence, informs us:

you think it makes you a fraud, the tiny fraction anyone else ever sees? Of course you're a fraud, of course what people see is never you. And of course you know this, and of course you try to manage what part they see if you know it's only a part. Who wouldn't? It's called free will, Sherlock.

We are constantly trying to manage how we are perceived by other people. We ingratiate ourselves, or we are standoffish, but both are about managing how we appear in the world and in the eyes of others. There should be some leeway for the grief-stricken. If, in rising to the daunting task of delivering a eulogy, they choose to rely on 'the words of another' as Matthew does in *Four Weddings and a Funeral*, we should cut them some slack. Conceding to convention and outsourcing sentiment doesn't make anyone a 'fraud.' Let's be tender.

But in the same breath we should also acknowledge that this habitual reliance on received ideas happens because raw and unprocessed emotion is unwelcome. To speak freely, to break down, to become illegible is to breach the etiquette of the contemporary eulogy. Consciously or not, this unspoken etiquette has come to govern how we speak about our loss in public. The need to be appropriate has come to outweigh the need to process. While there is no pure, authentic form of the eulogy to return to, our present over-reliance on cliché is an invitation to question the genre of the eulogy and the cultural conversation that largely sidesteps the topic of grief. Maybe by taking the extra time to distill emotion and to find our own words we can begin to peel away some of the especially callused clichés that have hardened around public grief.

Returning to the act of contemplation of one's own death, it seems to me that the desire to finesse the final words of one's life also veers toward the denial of death's inevitability.

Especially in the instance of Mailer's mock eulogy, there is a sense that making light of one's own death is – as any student taking Intro to Psych would tell you – a coping mechanism. This satirical wordplay of a eulogy helps Mailer, and maybe his reader, conceive of the abyss in slightly less terrifying terms. Once again, perhaps this can be forgiven. But effacing the emotional and existential fact of one's death might also be an unconscious response to the demand – prevalent in our society and on display in our popular culture – to deny death. The constant call to affirm life makes the situation and eventual reality of death a kind of embarrassment, a bad word: a topic we can only talk about with some parodic panache or in recycled platitudes.

Mailer's eulogy is a satirical assembly of crude arithmetic, but in its crudeness returns us to the divisions of property and inheritance that preoccupies the strategic planning we do for our own death. We are advised to plan for death mostly as a matter of accounting. One is encouraged to prepare one's last will and testament well ahead of time, to proactively arrange for the divvying up of property and the dispersal of objects. Consequently, property becomes the crucible of family dynamics, and, more often than not, it is where feelings of pain and grief's disorienting power get played out. Instead of reflecting on who will deliver our last words, time and money is spent on figuring out who will get our stuff. The loose ends of an estate, of capital distribution, become the focal point around a death in the days that follow it instead of a confrontation with loss.

One's death then becomes a matter of calculation: what was that life worth? How does it break down in terms of addition, subtraction, division? Inheritance is about keeping whatever wealth we may have accumulated in a lifetime in the family. That emphasis on wealth – especially in the form of property – and inheritance foregrounds the role of the state in our death. Like marriage, which sanctifies our sex lives and intimate desires before government, inheritance is a way of squaring our small lives in relation to that same government, making our individual ends a matter of legal rather than emotional interest. We can see how the redistribution of money is valued as an important matter to be attended to after a death, and also the subtle ways in which grief and mourning are deemed useless, auxiliary to public life.

When I returned to my small and nosy liberal arts college at the age of nineteen, after my mom died, the secretary told me she could sympathize: 'It's so much paperwork!' she lamented. I hated this woman for saying something so crass, so stupid. I hated her for not comforting me with better words than these, but I also hated her for being right. The overwhelming logistics of funeral planning and of dispersing the material traces of a life is exhausting. It also becomes the focus in the weeks proceeding death, the tangible and productive work that can be done. This work has a clear timeline, and it is a project that can clearly and effectively be managed, which makes it unlike the endless work of grieving.

In so many ways, death emphasizes over and over the fact that time doesn't work the way we think it ought to. We plan for things beyond our death as though that's a reasonable thing to do, and we impose linear plans onto its chaos (be it through a cued-up pop song or last-minute codicils). Trying to bring order to our abrupt end is futile, but that doesn't seem to stop anyone from trying all the same. Our careful calculations and plans, be they motivated by fear, or maybe egoism, can in no way outsmart, circumvent, or master the fact of death.

Ordinary Ruins

The October 29th entry in Roland Barthes's *Mourning Diary* – a journal he kept to document the elliptical sentences that came to him after his mom's death, and which was published after his own – reads: 'In taking these notes, I'm trusting myself to the banality that is in me.' What Barthes understands is that grief is boring. He also understands that it is worth trusting the banality of grief because something honest lies in its wrinkles and creases – what I think of, to borrow one of his lines, as 'the lineaments of truth.' Mourning, as I've said, holds very little entertainment value since it repeats the same story over and over (and over and over). Barthes recounts, 'One day, leaving one of my classes, someone said to me with disdain: "You talk about Death very flatly."– As if the horror of Death were not precisely its platitude!' The terror of death is just how boring it is, how positively certain and flat it is sure to be.

At the same time as Barthes was keeping a private diary – with entries like 'An onset of grief. I cry.' – he was also at work on a polished, publication-oriented work, 1980's *Camera Lucida*, where he undertook to theorize photography. He ruminates on what still images are, and what they do, and asks a central question: 'does photography exist?' In the midst of this theorization he also grieves. Barthes mourns his mother, Henriette, by describing the countless photographs of her he sifted through during her illness, and which he clung to after her death. *Camera Lucida* is an extended eulogy for his mother, insofar as it is an offering – some reflections on photography, yes, but also on time and extended sorrow. (That Barthes himself died shortly after its publication lends it elements of the self-penned eulogy, too – not unlike Bowie's *Blackstar* album.)

The pinnacle of Barthes's theory of photography (it does exist, after all) is formalized – or really, not formalized at all but felt as a *wound* – in what Barthes calls the Winter Garden photo, which depicts his mom as a young child. A master of the parenthetical aside, Barthes tells his reader that '(I cannot reproduce the Winter Garden photograph. It exists only for me. For you, it would be nothing but an indifferent picture, one of the thousand manifestations of the "ordinary" … in it, for you, no wound).' In his elegant way Barthes tells us that *we just wouldn't get it*, and he's right. We might look at the Winter Garden photograph and think, 'That's it?' or we might, as Barthes predicts, look at it as merely one of many 'manifestations of the ordinary.' We would see a young girl, a mere stranger, where Barthes sees the origin of his world. We could never see what Barthes feels when he looks at this picture.

For death really is the manifestation of the ordinary to everyone except the griever. Barthes's experience of looking at the Winter Garden image cannot be reproduced because his loss cannot be reproduced. If by merely looking at Henriette as a child we could feel what Barthes feels, grief would be translatable in a way that anyone who has grieved knows it is certainly not. Barthes describes looking through the many photographs of his mother as a 'Sisyphean labour' whereby he finds himself 'straining toward the essence' of her. He draws an analogy between this straining toward the essence in a photograph and having dreams of his mother – she is always there, but never quite. He dreams of her, but he does not *dream her*. The distinction might seem arbitrary, but it is not. He always falls short with this straining until he comes upon the Winter Garden image. The labour of mourning is much like this way of looking. We push the heft of our grief interminably upward and just when we think there might be some respite, or a pause in our loss, it rolls all the way back down and our mourning becomes as fresh as ever.

Grief is boring to those who peer at it from a distance. In grief we turn unapologetically inward, toward what we have lost and with little regard for who and what is still left, we indulge some narcissism and keep everyone else at bay, relegating them to the purlieu just beyond our private hurt. Narcissism has always been a slippery fish – flopping between a 'personality disorder' and a mere character trait, depending on who is doing the diagnosing. For our purposes, let's trace its two predominant meanings: narcissism is considered to be either excessive self-love and self-centredness or, it is, qua the *oed*, a 'condition of gaining emotional or erotic gratification from self-contemplation.' We might think of the first meaning in its emphasis on excess as akin to the prospecting for social cachet we find online when users grieve-post in thoughtless abundance, hoping to hit upon a viral nugget. The latter definition links narcissism to 'self-contemplation,' which is nearer to the work of private mourning.

This version of narcissism is also closer to Freud's original distinction, in 'Mourning and Melancholia,' between the healthy mourner who gets over his loss before too long and the mopey, narcissistic melancholic who doesn't. Narcissism, then, is derided as faulty because its inward gaze brings pleasure – even when that pleasure can be painful, as it is with grief. For Freud, and generations of practitioners after him, narcissism is a 'normal' part of development in childhood, but morphs into a psychological disturbance when it persists in adulthood. Yet there *is* a narcissistic pleasure to be taken in our grief – a self-centredness that can come as a relief. It can feel good to plug up your ears to the din of the outside world that continues to spin despite your loss. But this psychic sabbatical of self-indulgence too quickly gets chalked up to an 'unhealthy' egotism and the sojourn is cut short.

In *A Lover's Discourse*, Barthes describes what it is like to try to be normal when you're stumbling in the ruins of your loss. 'Sometimes I have no difficulty enduring absence,' he writes. 'Then I am "normal": I fall in with the way "everyone" endures the departure of a "beloved person."' Being 'normal' can feel like an endurance test, and it can often feel like the only socially viable option. I don't know where or when I learned that I needed to curb any narcissistic tendency I might feel, even in grieving, but I most certainly caught on quick. I recently found a diary I had sporadically written in the year following my mom's death. It makes my nerves itch to read it, not because of what it says, but because of what it so actively and assertively avoids saying. Even in the privacy of my own pages, I didn't let myself wallow in my loss. I wrote about everything except it. I wrote about the boy I was fixated on, about reading Melville, and – this is as close as I got to the truth – about how I was feeling a general sense of malaise.

It's no sin to be obsessed with dating and crushes at nineteen. I should give sad nineteen-year-old me a break. But then there is also a repeated refrain throughout the journal that seems impossible to believe at face value, and if I hadn't been the author of it myself I would be tempted to call it fake. In these pages, my younger self keeps wondering why I can't just be 'happy.' I keep wondering if art will be my path toward this elusive happiness, or if continuing to study literature will deliver the clap of inspiration I felt my life was missing. I wrote entry after entry confused about my sadness, as though the reason weren't right in front of me: I'd lost my mom and was trying to live on as if it was not so big a deal. I was pledging a clueless allegiance to a happiness script even in the gloaming of my grief.

There's only one entry where I allow myself some pity. On November 6, 2005, exactly one year after the death of my mom, I wrote:

> One year today. I sat in that room alone with mom until her sun-freckled chest stopped raising with the intake of air. We sat in the green hall on the cold floor in shock and relief and disbelief.

One year today and I feel hard. I'm cold and not able to grieve the way I want to. I want my grief to manifest itself outwardly so that I would have no choice but to tell the world. I'm sad, I'm lonely. I miss her.

I finally permitted myself some glum inwardness, some much-deserved narcissism that now I wish I'd allowed myself so, so much more of. I was wishing for a materialization of my grief – a permanent broken-heart-shaped bruise, an immovable mourning band laid taut against my puny arm, my brown hair turned white overnight – to signal my sadness to others. At the time I just couldn't find the words to articulate the grief that was engulfing me, and besides, I would have been too scared to utter them even if I'd found them.

To be overcome with grief is to have given a damn about someone else. To be narcissistic in your grief is to take the time you need to flounder in the new absence. In the wide expanse of newly discovered loss, we become situational narcissists, paddling in circles around ourselves, looking helplessly for what has already sunk. Narcissism is considered superficial and inauthentic, but that's only because we keep insisting it is. The insistence that narcissism and self-reflection are always already in excess of what is 'normal' is faulty – there is not *enough* introspection in modern life, especially when it comes to reflecting on death. In my own avoidance of processing the loss of my mom, I was, in a less obvious way, obsessed with it all the same. The energy I spent occluding my sadness was just as much work, I think, as it would have been to reckon with it. All I really wish is that I had been less concerned with my grief (and its attendant narcissism) imping-ing on the comfort of others.

Sifting through photographs, and theories of the photograph, Barthes wonders where death has gone and if it bears 'some historical relation with what Edgar Morin calls the "crisis of death" beginning in the second half of the nineteenth century... For Death must be somewhere in society,' Barthes muses, 'if it is no longer (or less intensely) in religion, it must be elsewhere.' He suggests that with the 'withdrawal of rites' and the wearing out of religious illusion, there is now an 'asymbolic Death, outside of religion, outside of ritual,' that has taken its place. Which is to say, death is no longer a site of meaning – of faith, of comfort, of value – but an abruptly literal thing. Since we no longer sit with death for very long anymore and since it does not get the same prolonged attention it once did, death becomes purely (and terrifyingly) literal, and a binary is entrenched between life and death, as though they weren't intrinsic to each other. For Barthes, death returns in the photograph: '*Life/Death*: the paradigm is reduced to a simple click, the one separating the initial pose from the final print.'

This return of death in the final print of the photograph sounds a lot like Freud's theory of the return of the repressed, which was later taken up and further theorized by Barthes's contemporary Jacques Lacan. Freud and Lacan write about how what we unconsciously repress (refuse to acknowledge, resolutely deny) comes back in other ways – against our will. In other words, we can't hide from what we don't want to see or feel. According to Freud, no taboo desire or traumatizing experience or nebulous fear is forgotten. Quite the opposite: these wishes and feelings and fears are almost immortalized in our unconscious minds and they are just biding their time until they surface again. We have come to repress death so assiduously and so often that it is bound to rear its head in ways we can't anticipate. So we can buy all the self-help books we want, we can continue to drape our illnesses in aggressive and death-denying language, and we can give clichéd eulogies instead of grappling with last words ourselves, but death isn't going anywhere. The repressed returns. Conventionally, the return of the repressed manifests in slips of the tongue, mistakes in memory, fantasies, and the like, but what Barthes's *Camera Lucida* suggests is that this return can take shape in our cultural productions, too – like the photograph.

'The *indescribableness* of my mourning results from my failure to hystericize it: continuous and extremely peculiar indisposition,' writes Barthes in his *Mourning Diary*. Written from October 26, 1977, until September 15, 1979, the book is revealing and banal in ways that *Camera Lucida* isn't. That's because Barthes wrote *Mourning Diary* for an audience comprised only of himself. He gave his grief the space to unfold and to expand into pages. Simply put, he felt no need to be entertaining. He finds himself unable to 'hystericize' his grief, and thus render it more recognizable, part of a more familiar narrative with arcs and twists and a denouement. Barthes, newly bereft of his mother, didn't worry about repeating himself too often; if a thought reappeared, he let it and he wrote it down. Barthes writes, 'this mourning of mine ... doesn't wear out in the slightest.' He allowed his thinking to be boring, and in this diary he made his grief the sole focus. This patient, inward turn results in some of the most poignant writing on grief there is.

Mourning Diary is everything the modern eulogy lacks: it takes its time – it does nothing more than stare at the shock of death in the wake of loss – it doesn't need to stand in front of an audience and deliver a speech; it says what it wants (embarrassing, angry, less than revelatory); it is repetitive. There is something vital about mourning to be gleaned from the uselessness of Barthes's diary. There is something universal in how minute and uneventful Barthes's grief is. What Barthes outlines philosophically about the tedium of grief we can see illustrated in Joan Didion's mourning couplet: *The Year of Magical Thinking* and *Blue Nights*. These non-fiction books were written on the heels of Didion's immense personal grief when, in the span of two years, she lost her husband, Gregory Dunne, and her only child, Quintana Roo. Her husband dropped dead right before dinner one night, and her daughter spent twenty-one months in different intensive care units, from California to New York City. 'Life changes in the instant. The ordinary instant,' writes Didion in *The Year of Magical Thinking*. The ordinariness, the quick, deep cut of loss, which happens in an instant and lasts forever – this Didion understands. Her paired memoirs of loss come as much-needed chronicles of the quiet shapes grief might take in our otherwise loud and bombastic world. Other than self-help books and French post-structuralism, where might we turn to model our grief? Where might we look for a little melancholic camaraderie? That's maybe why *The Year of Magical Thinking* is often sold on drugstore bookstands – Didion's story of loss has become a quotidian object because there is always someone, somewhere, buying a tube of toothpaste who is newly in the throes of grief.

Yet, as comforting as it was for me to find Didion's account-ing of ordinary loss when I did – and to hold in my hands a sustained and personal study of mourning – both books also seemed to hold the reader at arm's length. There is a stiffness to these texts I think comes from Didion's notion that even though grief is totally disarming, disorienting, and can feel at times fantastical, it is a process that ought to come to a clear end. 'I know,' writes Didion in *The Year of Magical Thinking*, 'why we try to keep the dead alive: we try to keep them alive in order to keep them with us. I also know that if we are to live ourselves there comes a point at which we must relinquish the dead, let them go, keep them dead.' Reading Didion, what I found was a view of death that wasn't so far off from the hoary and, I think, damaging Elisabeth Kübler-Ross–like model of grief marching along through its five stages. Didion grasps for a finality in mourning – a way of keeping the dead buried –

that feels too efficient to me. I don't want to relinquish my dead. (In defence of Kübler-Ross, her stages of grief were only the first part of a longer, much more thoughtful study, but they were taken far too literally by readers and practitioners looking for an easy, linear, fool-proof route to acceptance and grief's completion.)

While so many have found comfort in Didion's memoirs, I find myself chafing against the nonchalance with which her immense wealth comes out in her prose. She coats her suffering in a high-gloss veneer and occasionally seems stunned that her money did not protect her from pain. In *Blue Nights*, especially, Didion's memories of her daughter are tethered to the material objects of their family's wealth. The class privilege is so conspicuous here that she feels the need to 'lay this on the table,' as she says. Didion begrudgingly concedes that 'Quintana did not have an "ordinary" childhood … she was "privileged"' – unnecessarily encasing the word in quotation marks. This laying out of Quintana's privilege on the proverbial table reveals Didion anticipating readers with objections. '"Privilege" is something else,' she writes.

> 'Privilege' is a judgment.
> 'Privilege' is an opinion.
> 'Privilege' is an accusation.
> 'Privilege' remains an area to which – when I think of what she endured, when I consider what came later – I will not easily cop.

I find this passage maddening. In her rhetorical listicle, Didion decides that privilege is not the protection of an entire social and economic system that insulates the rich, but rather the realm of mercurial emotion – essentially, she likens privilege to a meritless concept, 'an accusation.' What Didion infers here is a belief that her privilege should have protected her and her kin from suffering. Hewing to her shock at the swift loss of her two closest beloveds is a secondary sense of shock, reverberating at a slightly lower register, that it had happened to *her* family. Despite her seeming capacity to understand the ordinariness of death even in the face of extraordinary grief, Didion feels the need to insist that privilege is a flimsy thing, a matter of opinion, and yet hers was so well-worn after years of use that she must have also thought it a sturdy second skin shielding her against catastrophe. '*This was never supposed to happen to her*, I remembered thinking,' Didion writes of Quintana in *Blue Nights,* 'outraged, as if she and I had been promised a special exemption.'

In the spirit of Barthes and of his mother, Henriette, I went looking through some photographs of my mom. I haven't looked much at photos of her since she died, and when I started my small archival dig I realized that most of them I had never seen at all. There is one photo in particular that, while I can't claim it as my Winter Garden equivalent, I found arresting. Susan Sontag writes in *On Photography*, 'Photographs, which cannot themselves explain anything, are inexhaustible invitations to deduction, speculation, and fantasy.' In my instance, this photograph came as a welcomed, even overdue, invitation to fantasy. The picture is slightly larger than your standard four by six inches, and it has become browned and crinkled with age. Tape that has long since lost its stickiness hangs off the corners of the photograph, with bits of paper still clinging to it from a scrapbook where the photograph once was kept. In the picture, my mom's body forms an arc as her right arm cuts vertically through the air with a tennis racket in hand while the left reaches out horizontally to help her balance. Only one of her feet has left the ground, but even then, just a little bit. She wears a full tennis getup: tube socks and white sneakers, a pleated skirt and Vneck cable-knit sweater with a button collar poking out from underneath (also all white).

I'm describing to you some of the details, and there are more I could give. I could give you some context, like the fact that my mom was the city tennis champ of Hamilton, Ontario, back in her day, or that she played varsity for her university. But, if I'm really to be in the spirit of Barthes's way of looking, his way of 'straining toward the essence,' then I'll admit that the astonishment of this image does not lie in the facts. What captures me is the blur of the racket as it swoops through thin air. The fuzziness of this part of the image shows a motion that was over the very next instant, and that reminds me just how long-over that instant is now.

I want to be able to strain toward an essence like Barthes does, but instead I look for my own likeness. I notice that her eyebrows thin out at the ends just like mine, which make them fade into nothingness when photographed. I see that her legs aren't quite my legs, but then I look at her hair, her eyes, her chin, and think about how I've been told my whole life that I am her spitting image. I can see it here. The part of the photograph that holds my attention the most and that my eyes keep returning to – what Barthes would call the *punctum* (the point in the image that pricks me) – is my mom's left hand. It is the only uncontrolled movement she makes: the fingers hold no pose, but are gently splayed in a blurry motion like the swoosh of the tennis racket. I never saw this picture when she was alive, and so the image holds meaning for me only in the fact of her death. I look at this glamour shot of my mom playing tennis sometime in the mid-1960s in Dundas, Ontario, and what I see is my own wish for her to fleetingly return to me. *Swoosh*.

But perhaps my Winter Garden photograph is not a photograph at all but a grocery list. For nearly twelve years I've kept a grocery list, twenty items long, that my mom had written out. She probably wrote it a few months before her death, and I found it in the pocket of a pink sweater I had bought her the previous Christmas. I've kept the list because I don't want to forget what her handwriting looked like. The small white square of paper now folds easily into its worn creases, made supple from years of repeated foldings and unfoldings. I like to look at the list because in her cursive hand my mom comes back to me. It's not just her handwriting I'm reminded of, but her trill little voice, singsong when she teased you, commanding when it needed to be.

The items on her grocery list (soy milk, tile cleaner, tuna) help me remember the routine things she liked – small preferences, the constellation of tiny decisions that made up her life. There is nothing remarkable about it, as far as grocery lists go. Why this scrap of paper holds what feels like a universe for me is because with her death I lost all the trivial things that made my mother, Pat, a multi-dimensional person, that made her alive instead of dead.

The Amateur's Art

I have always thought that *Proof*, directed by John Madden in 2005, is a film whose charms and insights have regretfully remained unsung. My allegiance isn't particularly to Madden's talents, nor to the play by David Auburn upon which the screenplay is based, and not even to the genuine appeal of its stars, the baby-faced Gwyneth Paltrow and Jake Gyllenhaal (such youth!). It's the script that makes this movie, about a dead mathematician (Anthony Hopkins) and his grieving daughter (Paltrow), more than a pastiche of dialogue and mood music, but a smart and honest snapshot of grief's ugliness. Auburn adapted his play to the screen with the help of Rebecca Miller (daughter of playwright Arthur Miller), who has become a formidable director in her own right. The anger that Paltrow's character feels in the wake of losing her dad rings true even though the feelings of frustration inherent to mourning are often obscured when they are dramatized for the sake of the box office (not coincidentally, *Proof* did not earn back its $20 million production budget in ticket sales). *Proof* does something else surprising – it indulges its grief-stricken protagonist in her fantasies.

Fantasy is an integral part of grief. Heftier than mere wishful thinking, fantasy is a mode of thought that can open a person up to her most buried desires or her unconscious wants. Fantasy acts as a mediator between reality and desire – a compromise for what we want most but which is impossible, or wouldn't go over well in the real world. Fantasy can crop up in the form of daydreams or episodes we recount in a waking state, and they can feel deceptively real. Imperfect though it may be, Joan Didion's *The Year of Magical Thinking* certainly gets that part right – the part where the mind, newly acquainted with the dark, endless rooms that grief brings with it, drifts into another fantastical register. For Didion, her year of letting her mind think magically, whimsically, brings comfort. Her irrational thought processes and constant free-associating lulls her into a calm that brings her late husband back to her in small but welcome snatches. What is compelling about *Proof* is its depiction of the other side of a griever's tendency toward fantastical thinking. That is, the moment when that calm of revisioning the dead gets punctured and feelings of peace are replaced by anger at reality.

Anger is deemed especially ugly when it's a woman wearing the grimace. Angry women are seen as 'unhinged' (as though we are unwieldy doors that need fastening) while male anger is conventionally understood much differently. Take the character of Dylan McKay from *Beverly Hills 90210*, if you will. Luke Perry plays teenage loner Dylan, who wears motorcycle jackets and broken-in denim with a bad attitude and a chip on his handsome shoulder. His absentee dad was in prison and then was later, it appeared, killed by the Mafia in season three. (Actually, he *wasn't*! But Dylan doesn't learn this until season ten, and so his experience of loss was real, even though the death was not.) The depiction of grief *90210*'s writing room came up with was a brooding and mysterious and *masculine* sorrow that lashed out against any offers of comfort. Dylan was always hopping on his motorcycle and buzzing off into the sunset like his kindred Hollywood doppelgänger, James Dean. Dylan's grief was kind of cool because it made him mysterious and emotionally bruised, with a tormented heart of black and blue. When a woman, like *Proof*'s Catherine, for example, acts out her heartsick anger, she is often condemned as 'hysterical,' in need of a long bath or maybe a nap. No one ever told Dylan to nap! Even when it stems from grief-stricken heartache, anger is seen as unbecoming on a woman and a sign of her mental instability, which, incidentally, is enough to drive her mad.

Proof opens with a scene of fantasy. Paltrow as Catherine ambles around her family home – surrounded by piles of books and other intellectual ephemera – when her father (Hopkins) arrives to wish her a happy birthday. He hands her a cheap bottle of bubbly ('I didn't know they made wine in Wisconsin,' she teases) and tells her things are going to look up for her – the slump she's been in for the last two years as she's nursed him in his sickness will not last. Moments later, after Catherine snags him in a logical inconsistency, he reminds her that he can say and do whatever he wants because he is *dead*. Catherine remembers aloud that her dad died the week before and from this realization she (and the camera) spiral back into earlier memories of her father when he was lucid and well. Though she is quickly jolted back into reality by the arrival of Hal (Gyllenhaal), the tone of the film has been firmly set: fantasy and memory offer a certain strain of comfort that reality fails to provide the griever.

Outside the realm of the fantastical, Catherine is mad as hell. When her sister Claire (played by Hope Davis) arrives on the scene, she is ruthlessly upbeat in the face of her dead dad and armed with to-do lists and tips for productivity. In this way, the movie subtly codes her as the repressed one, unable to engage genuinely with her loss. 'It's a funeral but we don't have to be completely grim about it!' she advises. When their father's funeral proceeds in a similar tone to Claire's chin-up attitude, Catherine's anger finally overflows and gets its voice in an unlikely place – an impromptu eulogy for her dad.

'I'm not on the program,' she begins, interrupting the small string orchestra as she takes the podium at the front of the church.

Wow. I can't believe how many people are here. I never knew he had this many friends. Where have you all been for the last five years? I guess to you guys he was already dead, right? I mean, what's a great man without his greatness? Just some old guy. So you probably wanna catch up on what you missed out on. Um... He used to read all day. He kept demanding more and more books. I was getting them out of the library by the carload. There were hundreds. And then one day I realized he wasn't reading. He believed aliens were sending him messages through the Dewey decimal numbers in the library books. He was trying to work out the code. He used to shuffle around in his slippers. He talked to himself. He stank. I had to make sure he bathed, which was embarrassing. Then he started writing nineteen, twenty hours a day. I got him this huge case of notebooks. He used every one. I dropped out of school. You see, he was convinced that ... he was writing the most beautiful, elegant proofs. Proofs like music.

I'm glad he's dead.

Though the final line makes it seem as though this might be the most heartless eulogy ever delivered, Catherine does not deface her father's memory by bringing up the harsh facts of his illness, or the truth of his abandonment by most people present at the funeral. Rather, she calls into question the very notion of legacy and of the art form of eulogy itself. When her dad fell ill, he was slotted into the category of 'already dead' by those who had known him as an indomitable academic force to be reckoned with. 'What's a man without his greatness?' Catherine asks, lambasting the way a person's worth is calculated (and how quickly it can move into a deficit). Catherine's eulogy is brutal and startling but it also points out with unwavering clarity that when the going gets tough, the colleagues, the acquaintances, the friends, and even some of the family tend to quietly get going.

If eulogies only ever speak to the accomplishments of the deceased – the prestigious stuff, the fancy titles, the charming habits – how are they any different than other happiness scripts we might unthinkingly follow? When Catherine makes mention of her father's stink, the embarrassment of bathing him, the aliens he thought were communicating with him, she makes evident the weaknesses of the old man, and the things that made him human. Those things aren't pretty, but they are true – and what's more, they also speak to the weight of loneliness and isolation Catherine herself felt as his sole caretaker in his waning years. Also an uncomfortable truth for others to face.

Even though this eulogy takes place in the reality of *Proof*, it also functions as a fantasy for the spectator to indulge herself in. And by 'the spectator' here, I mean me. Watching this B-list movie a year after I lost my mom, I took solace in the fantasy of having delivered an honest and angry eulogy of my own. I imagined pushing the family friend aside who spoke of my mom's newly discovered Christian faith (a last-minute garment she wore in the final few months of her life – like one might cling to a comforting blanket, devoid of any real healing properties, but still therapeutic). I would still speak of her accomplishments, which were many and distinguished, but I would also talk about her pain. I would talk about her night sweats and how she lost her hair at the back of her head first, where it rubbed against the pillow. I would curse the intolerably basic woman – a mere acquaintance – who hounded us in the last weeks of my mom's life for a lasagna dish she had left at our house. I would ask, like Catherine, where these rows upon rows of people had been for the last two years as my mom was eaten up by cancer. Some people very close to me would not be saved from my ire, and that would feel good, too. But as a spindly, very young woman who was relying on a self-prescribed dose of Gravol and Advil every night to fall asleep and rushing back to school in another province to write literature essays of no consequence, I was no Catherine. Perhaps that's why watching this grief-addled daughter lose her cool and speak so frankly about her hurt, and about the abandonment her parent must have felt during his dying days, was exhilarating. She enacted my own fantasy of eulogy revenge.

When Sally Field loses her daughter Shelby (played by Julia Roberts) in *Steel Magnolias*, Herbert Ross's 1989 Louisiana tear-jerker, she is, like *Proof*'s Catherine, pissed off. Though the film begins not with Shelby's funeral but with her wedding day. Amid the taffeta and big hair, Shelby's eventual death is quickly prefigured when she nearly collapses into hypoglycemic shock, a consequence of her type 1 diabetes. The wedding goes on, and a pregnancy soon follows, which delights Shelby but distresses her mom, M'Lynn (Field), who knows that childbirth could cause complications, potentially fatal, with her daughter's condition. Doe-eyed and already wistful about her unborn child, Shelby tries to reassure M'Lynn by saying, 'When all is said and done there will be a little piece of immortality, with Jackson's good looks and my sense of style.' Even though a baby is not in fact a piece of immortality, but rather another piece of mortality, Shelby has romanticized the idea of offspring as her living legacy. 'I'd rather have thirty minutes of wonderful than a lifetime of nothing special,' she muses.

Kidney failure eventually fells Shelby after a year of wonderful with her new kid. It's then, as M'Lynn sits helpless next to her daughter's hospital bed, that the audience witnesses the mother's angry grief percolating. M'Lynn holds a family picture up to Shelby – now hooked up to life support, with shorn hair and pallid flesh – demanding that she respond, despite being comatose.

When Shelby dies, M'Lynn is confronted with platitudes of sympathy that only enrage her more. Daryl Hannah plays a naive, god-fearing aesthetician who approaches M'Lynn as she stands next to her daughter's flower-clad coffin and informs her that it should make M'Lynn 'feel a lot better that Shelby is with her King.' With righteousness, she adds, 'We should all be rejoicing.' Issuing superb cut-eye, M'Lynn responds, 'Well, you go on ahead. I'm sorry if I don't feel like it, I guess I'm a little *selfish*. I'd rather have her here.' M'Lynn's heartsickness is visible all over her face and yet she still has to justify her grief, apologizing (however sarcastically) for indulging in her sadness. In offering her words of supposed comfort, the aesthetician makes an unequivocal demand of M'Lynn to be happy at her daughter's funeral. Her sympathy is cloaked in religious language, but the injunction is laid bare: M'Lynn should be 'rejoicing' instead of mourning.

Like Catherine with her eulogy in *Proof*, M'Lynn performs a fantasy of funeral free speech that doesn't quite exist in the real world. Leaving her daughter's grave after the funeral, she turns on her best friends – a dream cast of Dolly Parton, Shirley MacLaine, and Olympia Dukakis – and lets it all out. 'I feel fine,' she says when asked how she's doing.

> I feel great. I could jog to Texas and back, but my daughter can't. She never could. I am so mad I don't know what to do. I want to know *why*. I want to know *why* Shelby's life is over. How is that baby ever going to understand how wonderful his mother was? Will he ever understand what she went through for him? I don't understand. Lord, I wish I could. It is not supposed to happen this way. I'm supposed to go first. I've always been ready to go first. I can't stand this. I just want to hit somebody until they feel as bad as I do. I…just want to hit something…and hit it hard.

From here the scene devolves into a bit of slapstick, Dukakis's character offering up MacLaine as a cathartic punching bag, and they all end up in stitches from laughter. Although this ad-hoc eulogy is quickly resolved by humour (and the absurdity of trying to absolve M'Lynn of her grief by hitting her close friend), it is a flash of funeral misdemeanour that appeals to me. While M'Lynn does not deliver this impromptu eulogy before a large audience, her words function much the same as Catherine's in *Proof*. Both exhibit a latent wish to be able to say whatever one might want to in a eulogy. The reason we can't, and the reason we don't speak these truths, is because they are ugly and hard to hear.

Recent affect theorists have taken up the mantle of 'ugly feelings' (to filch affect theorist Sianne Ngai's useful phrase) such as grief to show the ways in which what we think of as 'uncomfortable' emotions reveal multitudes about the restrictiveness of living and feeling in the modern world. Following in the tradition of Eve Sedgwick – who championed an emotional and hopefully healing approach to knowledge, or 'reparative hermeneutics' – Sara Ahmed and other contemporary theorists of bad affects have argued that in North America today, feeling bad for too long is understood as a character flaw and a vice. Those who dwell in their shame, grief, anger, or despair are understood as self-indulgent narcissists who can't for the life of them find the bootstraps to pull themselves up by.

It is perhaps no wonder that we regularly repress loss and bury our unattractive grief-anger when death comes knocking. It is also little wonder that these thinkers are all working out of the discipline of queer theory – since queerness manifests (at least in part) as a mode of being in the world that doesn't make sense to the heteronormative status quo. Illegibility, incoherence, and perceived troublesomeness are part and parcel of queer identity as it has taken shape in discourse and practice since the 1980s in America.

In her recent work *Depression: A Public Feeling*, Ann Cvetkovich writes a paean to feeling down:

In investigating the productive possibilities of depression, this book aims to be patient with the moods and temporalities of depression, not moving too quickly to recuperate them or put them to good use. It might instead be important to let depression linger, to explore the feeling of remaining or resting in sadness without insisting that it be transformed or reconceived. But through an engagement with depression, this book also finds its way to forms of hope, creativity, and even spirituality that are intimately connected with experiences of despair, hopelessness, and being stuck.

Along these lines, might the eulogy – an inherently anxious genre – benefit from avowing its fundamentally depressive state? Instead of using the eulogy to laud the dead for her contributions to the collective, what if instead we forgave her for her faults? I like to think that if we explored 'the feeling of remaining or resting in sadness,' as Cvetkovich suggests, we could find a new way of living with the grief that will surely one day find us. If speaking the truth about the deceased's final days and his struggle weren't so taboo, maybe more people would stick around when that going began to get tough. It is a macabre sort of fun to watch angry women implode onscreen, but a better solace still could come from making those fantasies of free speech a reality – albeit in a slightly less volatile register.

Speaking of death is hard and eulogizing is a spectacularly failed art. 'Please excuse my papers,' said Cher in the opening lines of her eulogy for her ex-husband and co-performer, Sonny Bono, on January 9, 1998, in Palm Springs, 'but I've been writing this stupid eulogy for the last forty-eight hours.' Cher, ever a conduit for the truths of our time, touches on a central problem of the genre. Eulogies are frustrating to write and, yes, they are kind of stupid. Cher excuses her papers as though she should have been able to recite her eulogy; as though *reading* the words she wrote on the pages in front of her would dilute the message; as though recitation must signify 'from the heart' and reading would exemplify some sort of infidelity to the dead. Where does it say, I wonder, that you must deliver a eulogy off the cuff or from memory?

Cher is not alone in this assumption. Jacques Derrida, in eulogizing his friend and fellow philosopher Louis Althusser, also begins by apologizing for reading his prepared speech. 'Forgive me, then, for reading,' says Derrida, 'and for reading not what I believe I should say – does anyone ever know what to say at such times? – but just enough to prevent silence from completely taking over.'

This pressure to conform to the unwritten but acculturated rules of funeral decorum says a lot about what's wrong with the conventional eulogy. Here, Derrida also points out that there seem to be words that one ought to say at a funeral – presumably the clichés about heaven gaining another angel, a life fully lived, a candle extinguished too soon, etc. – and that no one (even those who fall into cliché) really has the right words for the occasion of death. It should come as some comfort to the rest of us to know that not even Cher, a multi-platinum songwriter and performer, and not even Derrida, one of the most eminent minds of the twentieth century, was able to 'find the words' to eulogize people they loved. It should come as a comfort because it confirms that eulogizing is at its absolute core an amateur's art. To approach it as such – with room to speak ungroomed thoughts and to voice ugly or artless feelings – might compel us to reckon with the unequivocal centrality of loss in our lives.

What sort of cruel joke is it, then, that we know loss in some primal way, but can't seem to talk about it? Both Cher and Derrida apologize for reading from papers, awash in performance anxiety, resentment, and, of course, the thick film of their own sadness.

The Big Lebowski, directed by Joel Coen and released in 1998, takes the amateur art of the eulogy to a purposely ridiculous – and cathartic – extreme. The eulogy that John Goodman as Vietnam War vet Walter delivers upon the death of bowling partner and friend Donny (Steve Buscemi) is a parody of the ritual and pomp that surrounds the very idea of eulogizing. Walter's oration style – registering somewhere in between a Cicero impersonation and a bad improv show – makes the rigidity of the traditional eulogy glaringly obvious. Having transported his friend's remains in a coffee canister because the mortuary tried to charge him $180 for an urn – 'It is our most modestly priced receptacle' – Goodman stands on the edge of the cliff with the Dude (Jeff Bridges) and begins the lofty work of eulogizing.

What follows is a summation of Donny as 'a good bowler, and a good man' who died, 'as so many of his generation, before his time.' Unable to resist the pull of tried and true last words, Walter usurps the lingo of war commemoration: 'In your wisdom, Lord, you took him. As you took so many bright flowering young men, at Khe Sanh and Lan Doc and Hill 364. These young men gave their lives. And so did Donny. Donny who loved bowling.' Flailing for the right words, Walter falls back on the language of death he already knows. He speaks of Donny as though he were a soldier killed in battle instead of a man whose heart suddenly gave out in the parking lot of his favourite bowling alley. Walter resorts to the grandiose language of military sacrifice not out of disrespect for Donny, but rather, honestly enough, out of a lack of imagination. In closing, Walter remains consistent in his posturing toward tradition. He concludes: 'And so, Theodore Donald Kerabotsos, in accordance with what we think your dying wishes might well have been, we commit your final mortal remains to the bosom of the Pacific Ocean, which you loved so well. Goodnight, sweet prince.' (Nothing like a little *Hamlet* to class it up.)

The scene's absurdity foregrounds the question of who the eulogy is for and the ways in which it is a debased art that is doomed to fail. Gesticulating like a drunk pastor, Walter tries to invoke a formality that feels comically out of place at this particular ceremony. If being stuffed into a coffee canister weren't proof enough of the lack of pomp for poor ol' Donny, when Walter empties the vessel – with the intent of spreading the ashes into 'the bosom of the Pacific Ocean' – the wind catches and sprays the gritty soot over the Dude, cloaking him in a fine coat of burnt human remains. So Walter fucks up, but he's sorry, and he knows the Vietnam part was bad. He says they should go bowling.

The next shot of the glint of the high-gloss lanes, the curved tops of the pins awaiting their future fall, reads like the eulogy Walter wasn't quite able to deliver. *The Big Lebowski* doesn't present death or mourning as hilarious; it underscores how easily, and even with the best of intentions, we can fumble someone's last words. The Coen brothers' film doesn't laugh at sorrow – it mocks the bombastic ways we have come to pseudo-grieve, and it suggests through parody that these performances are worse than silence because they ring so hollow. Walter's eulogy is amateurish and off-key. Cher and Derrida also express anxiety about the inadequacy of their words, about being novices. But who would want to be an expert eulogizer? What lonely work that would be.

The first eulogy I can remember hearing was the one delivered by my dad when his mom, Dorothy Cooper, died in Smith Falls, Ontario. He quoted a more appropriate passage from Shakespeare than *The Big Lebowski*'s Walter, he thanked people in the audience for coming – mentioning how certain people were connected to the family – and recounted the story of when Dorothy had let her three boys bring home an orphaned chicken, Olive, from the local dump. My dad explained that Olive's homecoming was exemplary of my grandma's kindness. What my dad did for his mom was a final act of love, and while it revealed to me parts of Dorothy I hadn't known first-hand, it also revealed to me my dad as a grieving son doing his best to bring warmth to the story of my grandma's not always easy life.

Mourning Althusser, Derrida admits that he doesn't 'have the heart to relate stories or to deliver a eulogy: there would be too much to say and this is not the right time.' Even though the funeral is traditionally exactly the right time to 'relate stories' and certainly to 'deliver a eulogy,' Derrida has a point. The form of eulogy as we know it doesn't leave room, doesn't make space for the time, to say all the things you might want to about your loss. As such, Derrida's non-eulogy is a great eulogy, much like Cher's frazzled eulogy is a sweet and honest eulogy. Not only because both philosopher and singer each mourn a unique individual, but because their words are also prompts for us to question and consider why we smush the work of collective and public mourning into a short address on a single day.

Even Cher, born for the spotlight, falters in the moment of eulogy. She wobbles between talking to Sonny and talking to his mourners, and drifts in and out of memory. She says that giving this eulogy is the hardest thing she will do in her life, and that's not because she has to stand up and deliver it while still reeling from her loss, but, I think, because it means closing the open tab of Sonny's life once and for all. She talks about the first time she met Sonny. She talks about the effect Sonny had on her until-then small world. She mourns herself – like we all do in grief. A part of us (or better maybe to say a *version* of us) is lost with the dead. We grieve a moment in time and place that will never be again, and so, by extension, a version of ourselves that existed in that space. I thought I would have a mom my whole life, I thought I would nurse her when I was old enough to be wise and old enough to know how to nurse the sick. I thought my mom would retire at sixty-five and spend her twilight years sipping Cabernet with girlfriends. I thought the biggest trials of my twenties would be finding a boyfriend and getting into grad school. My mom was so loving, and so consistently a stalwart of that love, that, to be honest, I *hadn't* planned a future distinctly with her in it because I hadn't considered any other possibility. Yes, I knew that she would die someday, but she had always been as immutable to me as the dark mornings in winter or the tendrils of steam that dance off a cup of hot tea – she and her warmth were just there, *obviously*.

Derrida says that when a friend dies our narcissistic tendency is to bemoan the interruption to our own lives and the bump in the road it has created along the path of our self-actualization. Each has his own memory of a person, and so we walk away from that person when they die, clasping our 'own little torn-off piece of history.' He speaks in terms of being swept up in the immensity of his loss because he is aware that he has lost a part of himself. But he's also more hopeful than that – he describes Althusser living on in him. We've heard this in the form of bromidic chestnut before – the dead live on within us, in their progeny, in our hearts always – but Derrida is getting at something a bit different here. He talks about losing the origin of the world in losing Althusser, not because Althusser was the centre of the universe but because he was an origin of the world as it existed with him in it.

The clearest and most stunning literalization of this some-what abstract concept of 'the dead within us' came to me like a punch in the stomach in a passage from Cheryl Strayed's memoir *Wild*. Recounting her three-month hike from the Mojave Desert to the Bridge of the Gods in Oregon, Strayed processes the loss of her mom ('the love of my life') with a gruelling honesty that can't help but be likened to the ugliness and sublimity of her physical journey. Strayed writes about spreading her mother's ashes, which for her, and for all of us who spread ashes or dump soil, was meant to mark a certain end to the grieving process. She describes her mom's newly carved tombstone with her name, the dates encasing her life, 'and the sentence she'd spoken to us again and again as she got sicker and died: *I'm with you always.*' She writes:

When we'd finally laid down that tombstone and spread her ashes into the dirt, I hadn't spread them all. I'd kept a few of the largest chunks in my hand. I'd stood for a long while, not ready to release them to the earth. I didn't release them. I never ever would.

I put her burnt bones into my mouth and swallowed them whole.

Strayed strains on her grief-stricken tiptoes to keep her mom close and to ensure the fulfillment of the promise carved on the grave. She makes literal what Derrida describes about Althusser within him. The ash and bones that Strayed swallows are her own little torn-off piece of history. 'I'd put her somewhere else. The only place I could reach her. In me.'

One of the most necessary things Strayed does in her memoir is this work of explaining the literalization of her grief. Not only by admitting her intimate incorporation of her mother's ashes, but also by showing how grief is embodied – literally, how it shows up on the surface of our skin and throughout the body. I say this is necessary because loss isn't an abstract 'labour' or simply a matter of the heart (there is nothing simple about it). In *Wild*, Strayed is able to relate how the embodiment of grief returns the body to its vulnerable, primal form. At a later moment out on the trail, Strayed recounts:

And then I wailed. No tears came, just a series of loud brays that coursed through my body so hard I couldn't stand up. I had to bend over, keening, while bracing my hands on my knees, my pack so heavy on top of me, my ski pole clanging out behind me in the dirt, the whole stupid life I'd had coming out my throat.

In these lines, Strayed describes the exhausting freedom of giving herself over to the animalistic pain of grief, of allowing herself to dissolve and become socially and linguistically illegible – a braying creature nearly on all fours. That she had to hike miles into an isolated wood in order to vocalize her overwhelming grief tells us something about how little room we make for mourning in our contemporary culture. If only there were a bit more room to disintegrate every now and again, maybe the alienation of loss wouldn't hurt quite so bad.

Recently, I sat cross-legged on dry autumn leaves before my mom's tombstone, looking at the dates of her birth and death separated by a short dash, 1947–2004. This little line was meant to represent a whole life, a synecdoche for all that transpired in her fifty-seven years whittled into an indent on a stone measuring only a few centimetres long. That short dash is insufficient for the myriad things it is meant to symbolize: the births, the lovers, a career, dear friends, silly anecdotes, her own grief, that time she mistook a rat for a kitten in the middle of a Quebec City snowstorm and scooped it up in a warm (then horrified) embrace, the grandkids she won't meet, her Christmas lists and shortbread recipe, the scent of her favourite perfume, using lipstick to rouge her cheeks when she was in a rush, her endearing and long-standing allegiance to the music of Anne Murray. *A dash.*

At the bottom of the stone is the phrase *with us always*, but it is written in all capitals, which I like because it then reads as part promise, part command: WITH US ALWAYS. This declarative phrase is similar to the one engraved on Strayed's mother's tombstone, I guess because it is something grieving people often get carved into gravestones. What strikes me about these words is that it's an impossible promise that, as heartsick kids, my siblings and I needed to see permanently imprinted. We gave ourselves this promise of my mother being with us forever at the very moment that it was no longer true. Of course it's not meant literally, *with us always* is meant as comfort, it was meant to turn our dead mom into a benevolent ghost, with us in the shadows, somehow glowing into apparition though she has yet to appear.

The thing about *with us always* is that it's actually quite a lot of work on the part of the grievers. Keeping the dead with you requires this constant living on with loss. *With us always* is arduous emotional work – *it's exhausting* – and it takes up a hell of a lot of psychic space. Keeping the dead flickering alive within us can require such a concentrated turn inward that it can come at the cost of your remaining relationships. Maintaining a fidelity to your loss is demanding, but trying to forget will leave you lonelier than you were before.

Reading *Wild*, I found lines like this next one, which made me feel as though I was reading about my own mom: 'She'd come at us with maximum maternal velocity. She hadn't held back a thing, not a single lick of her love.' Strayed gives voice to so many things I had felt about my mom that the experience of reading her memoir was incredibly painful, and yet I devoured it like I'd finally found some morsels to feed my grief. I read with a hollow lump in my throat that was a composite of recognition of my own loss, gratitude for finding it outside of myself, and envy for not having written it. I sat in awe of Strayed's ability to find the words to articulate the enormity of her loss, of her willingness to go back to the hideous parts of her mom's illness, and the generosity with which she shared the embarrassments of being in her twenties, totally bereft, having lost her grip on reality.

I read *Wild* not knowing how she had done it. How was Strayed able to mould her anguished grief – with all its scales and warts on display – into this burnishing narrative I held in my hands? Did she finish her hike and set to work right away on a literary pilgrimage to her loss? It wasn't until I finished the book and read the acknowledgments at the back that I saw she hadn't just hung up her Danner hiking boots and set to work. Strayed had fifteen years separating her from the end of her revelatory trip up the Pacific Crest Trail and *Wild*'s first draft. She needed the dust of her grief to settle, and, what came as comfort to me, she took the time that both she and her loss needed in order to bear proper, illuminating witness to it.

In some ways, losing part of ourselves in the death of one we've loved gets us back to the very start of all our relationships. Like the incorporation of ashes into our digestive tract, the movement of mourning always comes intimately back to us. What Strayed enacts on a literal level is true for the griever already, without needing to imbibe remains in an attempt to hold fast to the material world. The sense of loss we experience deep in our gut is not foreign, it is not alien. Yes, the dead are within us, but so are the living, who we will one day lose, too. Mourning is just a reminder that humans intuitively know loss more keenly than we know anything else.

Works Cited

Sara Ahmed, *The Promise of Happiness* (Durham, N.C.: Duke University Press, 2010).

W. H. Auden, 'Funeral Blues [1938],' *Auden: Poems* (New York: Everyman's Library, Random House, 1995).

Emma Barnett, 'How Did Michael Jackson's Death Affect the Internet's Performance?' *Telegraph*, June 26, 2009.

Roland Barthes, *A Lover's Discourse*, trans. Richard Howard (New York: Hill & Wang, 1978).

———, *Camera Lucida: Reflections on Photography*, trans. Richard Howard (New York: Hill & Wang, 2010).

———, *Mourning Diary*, trans. Richard Howard (New York: Hill & Wang, 2012).

Henri Bergson, *The Creative Mind: An Introduction to Metaphysics* (New York: Dover Publications, 2010).

E. K. Chambers, 'On Mr. Wm. Shakespeare, he died in April 1616 by William Basse,' *William Shakespeare: A Study of the Facts and Problems* (Oxford: Clarendon Press, 1930).

Geoffrey Chaucer, 'The Wife of Bath's Tale,' *The Canterbury Tales* (Oxford: Oxford University Press, 2008).

Anne Anlin Cheng, *Shine: On Race, Glamour, and the Modern* (PMLA: Publications of the Modern Language Association of America 126, no. 4, 2011).

'Commemoration, n.' OED Online, (Oxford University Press, 2016).

Ann Cvetkovich, *Depression: A Public Feeling* (Durham, N.C.: Duke University Press, 2012).

Henry Champion Deming, *Eulogy of Abraham Lincoln by Henry Champion Deming before the General Assembly of Connecticut* (Hartford: A.N. Clark & Co., State Printers, 1865; archived).

Jacques Derrida, *The Work of Mourning*, eds. and trans. Pascale-Anne Brault and Michael Naas (Chicago: University of Chicago Press, 2001).

Joan Didion, *The Year of Magical Thinking* (New York: Random House, Vintage, 2007).

———, *Blue Nights* (New York: Random House, Vintage, 2012).

Barbara Ehrenreich, *Bright-Sided: How Positive Thinking Is Undermining America* (New York: Picador, 2010).

———, 'Smile! You've Got Cancer' *Guardian*, January 2, 2010.

Helen Fielding, *Bridget Jones's Diary* (New York: Viking, 1998).

Four Weddings and a Funeral, dir. Mike Newell; perf. John Hannah, Hugh Grant, Andie MacDowell (Working Title Films, 1994).

Sigmund Freud, 'On Transience [1915],' *The Standard Edition of the Complete Psychological Works of Sigmund Freud* 14, ed. and trans. James Strachey (London: Hogarth Press, 1955).

———, 'Mourning and Melancholia [1917],' *The Standard Edition of the Complete Psychological Works of Sigmund Freud* 17, ed. and trans. James Strachey (London: Hogarth Press, 1955).

Vanessa Friedman, 'Prince's Heels Elevated Him as a Style Icon,' *New York Times*, April 22, 2016.

'Full text of Earl Spencer's Funeral Oration,' BBC News (archived).

Guinness Book of Records, ed. Craig Glenday (Guinness Media, 2009).

Phineas D. Gurley, 'White House Funeral Sermon for President Lincoln,' *New York Times*, April 20, 1865 (archived).

Love Actually, dir. Richard Curtis; perf: Liam Neeson, Hugh Grant, Emma Thompson (Universal Pictures, 2003).

Norman Mailer, 'Novelist Shelved,' *Boston*, September 1979.

'Narcissism, n,' OED Online (Oxford University Press, 2016).

Sarah Nicole Prickett, 'Hot Mail: "Heroes" Is a Song about Lovers,' *TinyLetter*, January 13, 2016.

Proof, dir. John Madden; perf. Gwyneth Paltrow, Anthony Hopkins, Jake Gyllenhaal (Miramax, 2005).

Raka Shome, *Diana and Beyond: White Femininity, National Identity, and Contemporary Media Culture* (Champaign: University of Illinois Press, 2014).

Zadie Smith, 'Fences: A Brexit Diary,' *New York Review of Books*, August 18, 2016.

'Sonny's Funeral, Cher Speaks,' YouTube, 2016.

Susan Sontag, *On Photography* (New York: Picador, 2001).

Steel Magnolias, dir. Herbert Ross; perf. Sally Field, Julia Roberts, Shirley MacLaine (TriStar Pictures, 1989).

Cheryl Strayed, *Wild* (New York: Random House, Vintage, 2013).

Colin Stutz, 'David Bowie's Death Leads to 100 Million Facebook Interactions in First 12 Hours,' *Billboard*, January 11, 2016.

Nicole Sully, 'Memorials Incognito: The Candle, the Drain and the Cabbage Patch for Diana, Princess of Wales,' *Architectural Research Quarterly* 14, no. 02, 2010.

The Big Lebowski, dir. Joel Coen; perf. Jeff Bridges, John Goodman, Steve Buscemi (Working Title Films, 1998).

John Urry, *Global Complexity* (Malden, M.A.: Polity Press, 2002).

David Foster Wallace, 'Good Old Neon,' *Oblivion* (New York: Little, Brown and Company, 2004).

Claire Wilmot, 'The Space between Mourning and Grief,' *The Atlantic*, June 8, 2016.

William Wordsworth, 'Sonnets from the River Duddon: After-Thought [1820],' Poetry Foundation, 2016.

Acknowledgements

The ideas and feelings that make up this book would not have come to see the light of day without my editor, Emily Keeler. A good editor makes her work invisible and Emily has performed the most magnificent vanishing act – but I still know, without a doubt, that this book belongs to us both.

My sincerest gratitude to Alana Wilcox of Coach House Books for her faith in this project and her devotion to weird and new ideas. Thanks must also go to the plucky Coach House Books staff past and present – especially Taylor Berry, Jess Rattray, and Norman Nehmetallah – for your unwavering excitement.

Many thanks to the talented Paul Terefenko for my author photo, and to Jocelyn Reynolds for allowing me to use her quiet storm of a photograph for this book's cover.

Thank you to my family and beloved friends for your profound and tender support – you have all promised to buy so many copies of this book before even reading a single line, and that's love.

Most of all thank you to my sweet husband and love of my heart, Tim MacLeod. Loving you is what I'm most proud of.

Julia Cooper has written for the *Globe and Mail*, the *National Post*, and Hazlitt magazine, among others. She recently completed a PhD in English Literature with the University of Toronto.

About the
Exploded Views Series

Exploded Views is a series of probing, provocative essays that offer surprising perspectives on the most intriguing cultural issues of our day. Longer than a typical magazine article but shorter than a full-length book, these are punchy salvos written by some of North America's most lyrical journalists and critics. Spanning a variety of forms and genres – history, biography, polemic, commentary – and published simultaneously in all digital formats and handsome, collectible print editions, this is literary reportage that at once investigates, illuminates and intervenes.

www.chbooks.com/explodedviews

Typeset in Goodchild Pro and Gibson Pro. Goodchild was designed by Nick Shinn in 2002 at his ShinnType foundry in Orangeville, Ontario. Shinn's design takes its inspiration from French printer Nicholas Jenson who, at the height of the Renaissance in Venice, used the basic Carolingian minuscule calligraphic hand and classic roman inscriptional capitals to arrive at a typeface that produced a clear and even texture that most literate Europeans could read. Shinn's design captures the calligraphic feel of Jensen's early types in a more refined digital format. Gibson was designed by Rod McDonald in honour of John Gibson FGDC (1928–2011), Rod's long-time friend and one of the founders of the Society of Graphic Designers of Canada. It was McDonald's intention to design a solid, contemporary and affordable sans serif face.

Printed at the Coach House on bpNichol Lane in Toronto, Ontario, on Rolland Opaque Natural paper, which was manufactured, acid-free, in Saint-Jérôme, Quebec, from 50 percent recycled paper, and it was printed with vegetable-based ink on a 1973 Heidelberg KORD offset litho press. Its pages were folded on a Baumfolder, gathered by hand, bound on a Sulby Auto-Minabinda and trimmed on a Polar single-knife cutter.

Series editor: Emily M. Keeler
Cover photograph: *Stasis* by Jocelyn Reynolds
Author photo by Paul Terefenko

Coach House Books
80 bpNichol Lane
Toronto ON M5S 3J4
Canada

416 979 2217
800 367 6360

mail@chbooks.com
www.chbooks.com